UNTOLD SOCCER SECRETS: AN INSIDE LOOK AT US YOUTH SOCCER

Dear founder of Stefano's fan club,
I hope this book finds you well. Big thanks
to Paul & Tom for making this possible. I'm glad
our paths have crossed again in some fashion.
I hope you're doing well in what you're
striving for. Best of luck with everything going
forward Will.

Cheers,

[signature]

WRITTEN BY

BRYAN MUNIZ
STEFANO MUNIZ

This Book is dedicated to:

God

The Muniz Family

The Titans Family

The Pollicino Family

The Morhmann Family

The Krongold Family

The De Macedo Family

Everyone inside the Stefano's Training Systems Family

The Velaszquez Family

Rest in Peace Adrian Velazquez

For soccer training in New Jersey, you can reach me

at

stefanostrainingsystems@gmail.com

@stefanostrainingsystems on instagram

Stefano's Training Systems on Youtube and Facebook

Table of Contents

Introduction

This book is a collection of information and experiences that aims to help players, parents, and coaches improve soccer for everyone involved. Inside this book, the reader will find all the essentials to becoming a better soccer player faster, and an authentic experience of someone who endured various challenges in soccer. The book is broken into two parts; Part I is a manual for breaking down and working on the game. Part II is what my father and I went through inside of youth soccer and some of the different things that parents and players will have to overcome together.

Before you begin, the information in this book means absolutely nothing if the person reading this doesn't attach joy for soccer to the core of being part of soccer. Soccer should be thought of as a platform for laughs, memories, and something that brings people from all walks of life together before anything else. Secondly, soccer should be a catalyst for someone to; learn how to learn, develop character, and a way to express oneself.

If you're interested in speaking with me, you can reach me at
stefanostrainingsystems@gmail.com

Part I:

The Essentials To Becoming a Better Player Faster

Chapter 1: Soccer Lifestyle

The difference in levels of soccer is how dedicated a player is to the game. If a player is motivated to become the best player they can be, it is essential that they adopt a soccer lifestyle. Adopting a soccer lifestyle is more than playing and watching soccer. A soccer lifestyle is when an individual focuses time and effort in all areas of life to be a better player, whether it's ordering something healthy when going out to a restaurant or not staying up late and making sure they get the proper rest to be able to train the next day. The individual maintains focus on becoming a better player on and off the field. By adopting a soccer lifestyle it accomplishes; learning how to learn, how to focus on something one is passionate about, and the work ethic necessary to be successful in anything.

Living a soccer lifestyle doesn't guarantee that a player will be successful, but it arms them with the best chance they have at excelling, and in the worst-case scenario it gives them life long lessons that can be applied to anything that they might otherwise not have obtained. This discipline is for individuals that love the game and have the motivation to become better. You can't want to be the best player you can be, while every action you take isn't in line with what you're trying to obtain.

If you're passionate about becoming a better player I encourage you to examine the information in this book with the joy of soccer in your heart, and recognize that the pursuit of becoming a better player is worth only as much as you enjoy playing. There will be a lot of bumps in the road, really good days, and really bad days. The only way to overcome and get through everything a player will go through, is to have an extreme joy for the game.

Chapter 2 A: Why becoming a technically proficient player comes first.

To win in soccer you have to score more goals than the other team. One of the things people don't talk about enough is that if you have the ball the other team can't score. Being a technically sound player is the foundation of being a great player. If you look at all of the top players, what is always a noticeable attribute is their control over the ball and the skills they have that help maintain possession and attack the other team. If being more athletic was the key to victory in soccer top-level teams would do what the NFL does and try to find the biggest, strongest, and fastest players. That is not what we see in soccer, as one of the best of all time, Lionel Messi, stands at 5'7. It is easier to become a better athlete than it is to acquire skills to control the ball and create attacks. Players at the youth level should focus on the skills necessary to maintain possession against a live opponent and the concepts that allow them to use their skills to create opportunities.

To acquire skills in any activity the individual must repeat the same movements until the movement is second nature. When a player begins soccer, you can see the time it takes them to recognize the situation they've found themselves in, and the time it takes for them to develop a command that corresponds with the situation. Possession is lost when the command that solves the situations isn't executed in time. To begin becoming a technically sound player it is important that the individual repeats the movements necessary to control the ball and make decisions quickly. The basic elements of controlling the ball and attacking successfully in soccer are; dribble, pass and shoot.

Dribbling is the foundation of possession. If a player can't dribble they can't be successful in soccer. Every successful play comes from the ability to make a controlled first touch and be able to navigate the ball away from defenders if needed. Dribbling can be broken down into three parts; first touch, ball retention, and attack dribbling. Within each of these components, how someone would work on them varies based on their current skill level. There are three different levels.

The first level of developing skills entails the constant repetition of the same movement until an individual can do the skill without having to consciously think it through. An example would be a player trying to control the ball with a first touch. At first, the player will have to keep in mind several details to control the ball and try to execute it while reacting to the different pace, height, and spin of the ball. Through constant repetition of receiving passes and controlling the ball, a player will eventually control the ball without having to think about it. This is a beautiful thing because now the player can focus on what comes after initially being able to control the ball.

Level two is where things get interesting. Inside this level, a player has developed their skills and are able to perform skills successfully without any pressure. Once a player can perform skills without any pressure successfully it is time to add concepts for how to use the skills to create time and space to relieve the pressure of an opponent that is attempting to make a tackle. An example of this skill being performed is taking a first touch that guides the ball into a pocket of space away from a defender that is advantageous for you and harder for the defender.

Level three comes after you are able to successfully control the ball with and without pressure. To get to an even higher level or even the highest levels of soccer requires players to play with a faster speed of play. A great idea that I'm sure we can all resonate with is; if I am going to race someone and want to beat them, but they are a lot faster than I am how can I still win? The only way possible is to cheat and get a head start on them. In soccer, we can apply this idea of getting a head start on our opponent by knowing what is going to happen next before the defender. This is what level three is all about; knowing what is going to happen way before my opponent and having the skill and awareness to execute my ideas faster than my opponent can react. An absolute golden nugget from this book is this; the defenders' ability to defend is based on how well they can react to what you are doing, based on what they have seen in the past. If a player can know what is around and what they want to do before they get the ball and can execute it successfully, the job of being a defender becomes a miserable task. Once a player can enter level three that's when the real fun of the game can begin.

Chapter 2 B: The most important touch in soccer, The first touch.

Control the ball, control the game. - Stefano

Every attack in soccer comes from being able to control the ball. If you can't control the ball you can't dribble, pass, or shoot. If that's the case what is the point of playing. Being able to control the ball is what separates being an athlete from a soccer player. The control of the ball is a skill that takes thousands of repetitions, control of your own body, and the understanding of how to use it. To shorten the time a player spends inside level one of developing a skill, they can use more effective means of training. For example, if a player wants to work on first touch control thousands of times it would be tough for them to find a partner to do all those repetitions with willingly, but it is a lot easier to find a wall that you can strike the ball against. I am a big fan of getting the most out of my time and effort. The more something is efficient and effective the better I sleep at night knowing the time and effort I spent didn't have a single moment of waste. Using a wall to develop the first touch is one of the best ways available because you are working on a number of things at the same time, while working on what is most important, control of the ball. The best feature of this method of training is that you can constantly vary the difficulty using different aspects you are looking to train.

As you begin training with hitting the ball against a wall it is important to consider different parameters to formulate the exercise for what you are trying to accomplish. To begin, the player must start off with proper soccer posture; feet shoulder-width apart, balanced, knees slightly bent, and chest leaning slightly forward with the back straight. This is very similar to the stance one would take right before pushing off the floor and jumping into the air. From this posture, everything in soccer is displayed whether it's running, jumping, or changing direction, dribbling, passing, or shooting. It is important to practice having the correct soccer posture because it is the foundation of all skills and movements in soccer.

Once soccer posture is being employed, a player can work on striking the ball and having it rebound back to them. As the ball rebounds back it is important to keep in mind the different ways a first touch can be used in soccer. You can use the first touch to stop the ball dead or move it in any direction by cushioning the ball and guiding it. The analogy I use when training players to have a good first touch is; what takes place when you are trying to catch an egg? Do you let the egg simply clash against your hands as they remain stagnant, or do you ease the velocity of the egg by cushioning the egg as it comes towards you? The ball needs the same effort of cushioning, but with our feet. This is something my father drilled into me. He would express that the cushioning of the ball came from bringing the knee up and swinging the lower part of the leg from the knee to the foot, backward as the top part of the leg stayed in the same place. I can still hear him in my head yelling "recoil!" every time a ball comes to me. To direct the ball in different directions you need to still cushion the ball but not completely killing the velocity to where the ball stays in one place after. The trick is to ease the velocity of the ball while using your foot to guide it into the space you need it to go in with the little velocity left from controlling the ball. This can be done while moving or standing still.

When practicing your first touch with a wall or partner, keep in mind how the skill will hold up in a live game situation as a defender applies pressure. As you develop the ability to make a good first touch, begin trying to use the first touch to create more time and space while you play. For example, if you receive a pass, and a defender is running straight at you, that means there is space to either side of the defender. As the defender approaches push the ball to the side of the defender, if the defender is coming in with a lot of momentum, the first touch to the side will beat them and break their momentum as they chase the ball.

The different ways a player will have to receive the ball are on the ground, in the air, or a bouncing pass. The key concept of being able to control any of these three is to first identify the center of the ball. Once a player can lock onto the center of the ball as it is coming in, to place the foot behind it, or any other body part, and cushion the ball becomes easier. That is another golden nugget; identifying the middle of the ball when you are receiving the ball or striking the ball for a pass or shot. The center of the ball is the middle of the ball on the surface of where the ball is facing you.

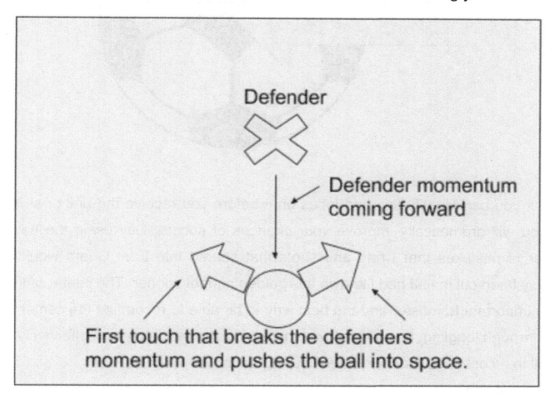

Exhibit A:

If you can identify this and focus on it before you receive the ball or strike the ball, you will dramatically improve your chances of successfully using the ball. The number of mistakes that I had and shots that soared into East Guam would have probably been cut in half had I known this golden nugget sooner. The center of the ball is very important to master and the best way to be able to recognize the center of the ball is through juggling. Juggling allows an individual to efficiently and effectively strike the ball in a controlled manner while focusing on the center of the ball.

Juggling is something a player should do every day whether if it's for a warm-up, cool down, or just to work on it because it is one of the best ways to work on so many things at once. To effectively juggle, a player can start with the ball either in their hands or from the floor if they are at a higher skill level. Once the ball is either dropped or popped into the air the player should try to focus on striking the ball with their ankle stiff as they point their toes down. From the shin to the toes should be one flat line as the player makes contact with their laces on the ball. A player can tell if they have executed a successful repetition if the ball travels in a straight line up and down and doesn't have any spin on it after the strike. I've named this method of juggling; power strike juggling. This beats most other methods because a lot of juggling techniques can fail to address striking and controlling the ball during the same repetition. When a player uses only the flicking of their toes on the ball to keep it up they are wasting time. This doesn't help strike or control the ball as much as power strike juggling and what can be done in less, is done more in vain.

To recap this segment of the book a player must get to a level of control with the ball where they can control the ball from the air, floor, or a bouncing pass without having to consciously consider every detail of the touch. As the player progresses, they should strive to use their first touch to create time and space to be able to effectively control and attack the other team's goal. Once a player can maintain possession with their first touch, playing the game of soccer begins as the person who is going to receive the ball can attempt to think steps in advance and see how they can disrupt the other team's ability to defend by playing with elements of deception and executing the rest of their play after they have successfully controlled the ball.

Control - Attack – Create

Chapter 2 C: You're going to have to try harder than that if you want this ball.

As I grew up playing soccer in an Academy in New Jersey, a common theme was that I was amongst the smallest players physically in both height and weight. To survive being bumped off the ball or getting the ball poked away by a bigger opponent, I had to develop a way to keep my balance while keeping the ball out of reach. This problem lead to the solution that would become the "Three-point System." The Three-point system is the most effective way to keep the ball no matter who is defending you. Here's how it works; the player in possession of the ball must first position themselves between the ball and the defender, creating a barrier with their body between the ball and the defender. Once the inside position between the ball and defender is obtained, the person in possession can use the foot they are dribbling with to then put the ball even further from the defender while maintaining possession. To put the icing on the cake, the player in possession can also put their arm out and bump into the defender with their arm either off-balancing the defender or offsetting how hard the defender can bump into you while you have the ball. When extending the arm it should not be swung at the defender or used as a strike. The arm being extended is a tool to put distance between the ball and the defender while also being able to feel the defender's balance and where they are applying pressure.

From the Three-point system, I was able to create my own playing style that helped me control the ball even against defenders who were a lot taller and outweighed me while playing high-level college soccer and being able to have solid performances in training sessions with professional players. In High school, I was so notorious for this that defenders would complain to the referee that I was obstructing them while I had the ball. This works in tandem with the first touch because you can take a first touch that allows you to position yourself in between the defender and the ball. If the other team doesn't have the ball they can't score, but you can. The Three-point system is the foundation of ball retention. Once a player can effectively shield the ball from a bigger, stronger opponent they can begin adding deception while implementing the three-point system. One of the best ways to dribble out of pressure is while maintaining the Three-point system; the player in possession of the ball uses a series of cuts that force the defender to reach around the shield you've created with your body forcing them to give up space while they are off-balance. This is seen in every high-level soccer game that you watch. Some players are more effective than others at this skill, but every player must have some ability to use this if they want to become a better player.

To work on the skills required to maintain possession of the ball, it is important that every player works on foundational exercises and gets them ingrained into their second nature, they are; boxes, in and outs, cuts, pulls, and scissors. The reason these are the skills that players must master if they want a strong ability to keep the ball is that they are able to practice these in a high number of repetitions, they make it easier to acquire other skills, and they work in tandem with the movements a player will have to perform when navigating the ball away from or past defenders. Once again, what can be done in less, is done in vain with more. One issue that has come about with social media is the delusion that doing complicated exercises and drills makes players better, but what complicated and low rep drills don't account for is the process of skill acquisition. I'll give you an example- if a player runs through an agility ladder then dribbles a couple of steps before shooting not only has time and effort been wasted, but the drill has done very little in making you a better player. If we compare the agility ladder shooting drill to a drill or exercise that has a player dribble 50 yards, and every 5 yards the player performs a series of boxes, scissors, or cuts, the player doing the 50 yards of dribbling while doing skills in between will have done thousands of reps more than the player who did two dribbles before shooting it. Who do you think gets better; the player who does two dribbles and shoots or the player who does hundreds of reps of a given foundational skill while covering 50 yards with the ball under control? I don't think the answer needs to be stated. Does covering 50 yards while dribbling and performing skills require a lot of grit? Yes, if you want to get better at something you have to exert effort. The thing that separates players is what they put their effort into. Let's say you have two individuals training to become better soccer players, they both put in the same time and effort, but one only works on shooting while the other works on controlling the ball after shooting it against a wall, does 500 juggles, and practices retaining possession of the ball using the foundational skills outlined in this book. Who is training more efficiently? The player who only worked on their shot, or the player who worked on everything from properly striking the ball, to properly controlling and retaining possession of the ball? Again no stated answer should be necessary. Though it seems like common sense, many players would much rather spend time shooting the ball in single repetition fashion into the net, rather than using their time effectively on the elements of soccer that would grant them the ability to get a shot off in a game in the first place.

Retention of the ball comes from first being able to control it with an advantageous first touch into space away from a defender, then having the skills necessary to wedge your body in between the defender and the ball effectively using the Three-Point System. The development of ball retention stems from consistently repeating the foundation skills of boxes, in and outs, cuts, pulls, and scissors. If you get to a high level of being able to execute these skills you will drastically improve your ability to keep the ball under pressure in tandem with the Three-point system.

Chapter 2 D: Dribble and Giggle

As I grew up watching soccer I was always more interested in paying close attention to the players who were more entertaining with their dribbling. There was something about being able to run at defenders with the ball, put a fake on them, and then blow past them like they weren't even there, that got me to fall in love with the ball. Players such as; Ronaldinho, Robinho, and Ronaldo had a major influence on me wanting to practice dribbling more than anything. As I grew up, I even felt like there were times that I enjoyed taking players on more than shooting to the point people would yell at me, "Are you trying to dribble it into the goal?" A couple of times I was able to. Not every player has to try to be the next Ronaldinho or Messi with their level of dribbling, but every player should have an arsenal of moves to effectively take players on one-on-one and be able to beat them. Even at the professional level it always amazes me to see a top-level player get into a situation where it is one verses one and they don't have the audacity to run at the opponent and try to create something. Players shouldn't run at defenders every time they get the ball, but having the ability to take off with the ball and go at defenders will add a dimension to their game that most players do not have.

There are two forms of dribbling around defenders that a dribbler can use to beat a defender; Fake and take or a flash move. A fake and take is a move based on how the defender reacts to the move you are doing to them. For example, if I dribble at a defender and stop followed by immediately accelerating, that move only works if the defender's reaction is to stop when I stop. A flash move, my favorite, is when you put a move on a defender and disregarding the reaction they have, you just hit the move and go. For example, using a scissor with one leg and pushing the ball past the defender all in one motion and continuing to dribble at top speed after you hit the move. Both of these forms of dribbling past defenders are important because there are going to be times when you really have to wait for the defenders reaction and if you attempt to just fly past them they'll be able to stop you, whether if it's because of the positioning of the defender, where the ball is on the field, or if you don't have enough momentum.

No one else on the planet will outline this part right here; the three best moves in soccer are; change of speed, change of direction, and the best of all being the pump fake, commonly referred to as pretending to blast the ball and continuing to dribble or pass. The ability for the defender to defend is based on how well they can react to what they assume is going to happen and if you can use deception along with great control, how is the defender supposed to stop you. For example, if you are dribbling near the box of the other team and a defender blocks your immediate path to goal, and you act like you're going to blast it anyway as the defender blocks a shot that never happens, you push the ball into space, you have now effectively dribbled past a defender and have time and space to attack the goal. If you want the skills to be able to dribble past defenders simply work on dribbling, stopping abruptly and accelerating immediately, changing direction while dribbling at fast speeds, and pretending to blast the ball and then touching it into a pocket of space and continuing to dribble. These three moves work in combination as well. For example, a dribbler can be running at top speed with the ball on the side of the field in the offensive third, closer to the other team's goal. As they approach the end of the field they can pretend to cross it, change direction, and change speed all in one move. If you watch the highlights of the best dribblers, a combination or single use of any of these moves with deception is what allows a player to dribble past a defender. Some players may choose to dress it up as more than what it is, but dribbling past a defender can be as simple as pretending to pass it to someone and making the defender stop to play defense while you continuing on the dribble.

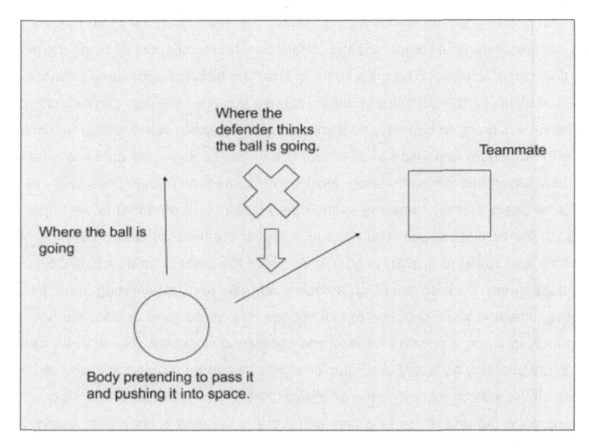

Where the
defender thinks
the ball is going.

Teammate

Where the ball is
going

Body pretending to pass it
and pushing it into space.

This next concept is going to be explained in even greater detail as we dive into the soccer IQ portion of this book, but it needs to be addressed in this section. If a player dribbles in a straight line directly at the other team's goal, the defenders will be able to address the dribbler and stop the initial direct threat of a dribbler going straight at the goal. If a player chooses to present an initial threat that opens up space for what the player actually wants, when the defender blocks the initial threat the player in possession can find the option they really want, that is playing the game of soccer. Soccer is being able to deceive the opponent and create the best opportunity possible to score more goals than the other team. For example, a player is dribbling at the other teams goal and if they try to pass it forward it'll be easily read for the defenders to intercept or make the pass harder to complete, but if the dribbler disguises their pass by acting like they're going to blast it and then turning it into a pass, the pass will be easier to complete because the defenders will be more inclined to assume the ball is about to be slammed forward rather than be passed on the ground. Opponents will block or brace for the initial threat of the shot while the real pass the dribbler wants to complete goes without being defended. If we can combine setting up what we want, while dribbling and selling the defender what we don't want, it'll be easier to fake out the defender and proceed.

Let's dive deeper into the mechanics and principles of dribbling past a defender with the context that we have the ball in space and it's a one on one situation. The first principle of dribbling is momentum. If a player is dribbling with speed at a defender, with the ball under control, the defender is immediately at a disadvantage. The defender is defending their goal but has to address the ball in front of them which forces them to face away from their goal. This puts the dribbler in an advantageous position because the defender has to then turn and start accelerating while the dribbler is facing the right way and can continue running at speed. If we use the analogy of two people starting a race, with one facing the finish line and the other facing away during the start of the race, the person facing the finish line will have the advantage of just being able to run straight forward while the other will have to first turn around and then start accelerating. As the dribbler approaches the defender they even have the greatest head start in the race to the goal because they're running forward and the defender still needs to turn and start accelerating as the dribbler has already been progressing forward with the ball.

Another reason the defender is at a disadvantage, is that while you approach them with speed, you force them to solve a problem faster than they have time to think about it. For example, if you ask someone basic math questions like one plus four, or three plus eight, and give them enough time to solve the question, they'll have an easy time solving the problem because they can think it through and come up with the solution. If you ask them the same math problems but drastically limit the time they have from one question to the next, it'll be surprising how the same questions they've previously answered are more difficult. This same effect of solving a problem with a limited amount of time occurs as the dribbler forces the defender to solve the problem with less time when the dribbler comes forward with speed. The difference between selling a fake or getting the ball taken away, is how well you convinced the defender with your body language.

Chapter 2E: Beat One Leg Beat The whole Defender

A concept that opened up my ability to dribble past someone is that if you dribble past one leg of the defender you can dribble past the entire defender. It seems logical, but when attackers approach a defender, you'll often see a look of "uh oh what do I do now?" across their face. A big misunderstanding happens when a player loses the ball on the dribble because a coach may say get rid of it quicker, when that wasn't the best option either. It's easy to just kick the ball forward, and not take the defender on, because in just kicking the ball away, you can blame any loss of possession on a miscommunication between you and your teammate, or make it appear like you were trying to do the right thing but just made an error. When you take a player on one-on-one, you will be held 100% accountable for your actions, which is an uncomfortable feeling. This discomfort is what makes players reluctant to work on their one-on-one skills. If you can use the concepts in this book however, you'll be having more fun playing, knowing that you were making the correct decision. It would mean that you had the audacity to take players on when the game required it, instead of being scared like most players.

Beat one leg beat the whole defender. I feel so strongly about this idea, that I couldn't wait to include it in this chapter. How does a player make sure they're just beating one leg when they dribble? How can they just pick one leg to beat on the dribble? I call this the midline principle, which states; if a player crosses the midline twice, they risk losing the ball to any half-decent defender, but if they only cross the midline once or get close to the midline before peeling out, they will only have to go through the trouble of dribbling past one leg.

What is the midline? The midline is a line between the center of the defender's feet in relation to the ball.

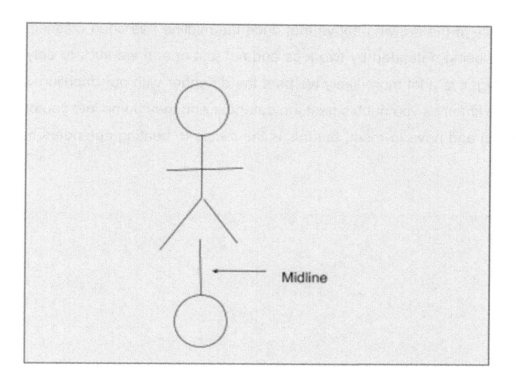

Understanding this is critical, as it will set you up for really understanding how to beat defenders. The rule of thumb is don't cross the midline twice.

Notice in the drawing above that once the midline has been crossed twice the ball is now being defended by two legs and not just one. If we stick to only dribbling past one leg, it is a lot more likely we beat the defender with our dribbling. There are going to be times as you dribble past the defender and they bump into you or you take a bad touch and have to reset, but this is the recipe to beating defenders more often than not.

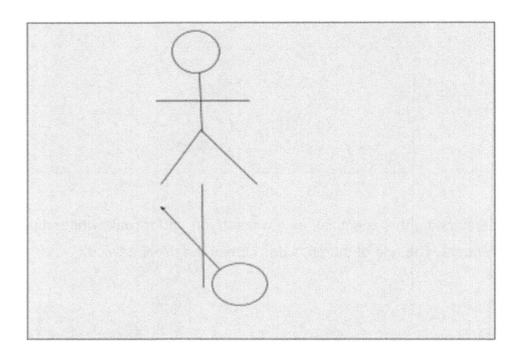

In this drawing, you can see that crossing the midline just once sets a player up to beat only one leg making it easier to beat the entire defender.

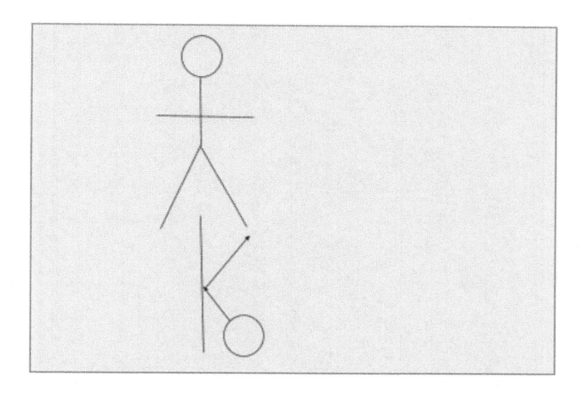

In this drawing you'll see that coming close to the midline and then going out to the side you're still only taking on one leg as long as you don't cross the midline twice.

Now that we understand beating one leg you beat the entire defender, we can address how to make beating one leg even easier. Let's consider the fact that as we try to propel our bodies in any direction while running, we need to load our body weight on our legs and push off to begin moving. When we dribble we can force a defender's leg to become loaded by making them feel the need to load their leg in preparing to propel themselves in one direction. When a defender is balancing on one leg, they have a harder time reaching for the ball.

Because the entire weight of the defender is on one leg, it leaves the defender planted and less able to challenge for the ball. They can only challenge for the ball as far as the leg without weight on it can reach which is usually insufficient when the ball is out of reach.

To effectively make the defender load their body weight onto one leg, attackers can use moves such as; body feints, scissors, and pump fakes. These moves have to happen quickly and be able to occur as you're dribbling at top speed. When an attacker is dribbling at a defender they need to keep their momentum while dribbling. When a player loses their momentum while dribbling, it makes it a lot harder to get past a defender.

Another principle that helps attackers get past defenders is "The in or out principle." The In or Out principle demonstrates that if an attacker can successfully display to the defender that they may either take off forward or cut in, it gives the defender too many things to defend. This sets the defender up to try to stop one, while falling victim to the other. This is further depicted in the drawing below.

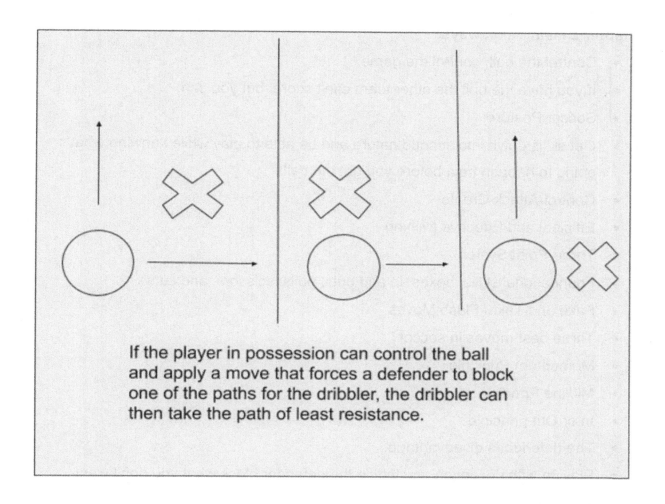

If the player in possession can control the ball
and apply a move that forces a defender to block
one of the paths for the dribbler, the dribbler can
then take the path of least resistance.

To become a better one-on-one player you have to experiment with what skills work for you, and keep working on them with and without an opponent present. If we look at Messi and Ronaldo, we can see that they both use different skill moves to go past defenders, but the midline, in or out, and momentum principles always remain true when they have success in one-on-one situations. The skills they use are usually some form of change of speed, change of direction, or a pump fake.

Chapter 2 Main Takeaways:

- Control the ball, control the game.
- If you have the ball the other team can't score, but you can.
- Soccer Posture
- Get skills down into second nature and be able to play while knowing what's going to happen next before you get the ball.
- Control-Attack-Create
- Efficient and Effective training
- Three-Point System
- Foundational skills: boxes, in and outs, pulls, scissors, and cuts
- Fake and Take/ Flash Moves
- Three best moves in soccer
- Momentum Principle
- Midline Principle
- In or Out principle
- The defender's disadvantage
- Playing with deception and letting the defender block what you don't want while making the play you really want.

Chapter 3: Passing

The game of soccer is won by scoring more goals than the other team. This doesn't mean we should attempt to rush the ball forward or shoot everytime we get the ball. In most positions on the field it doesn't make sense to shoot, because there are usually better opportunities that can be created. If a shot isn't worth taking when receiving the ball, the next best thing is a pass. The ball travels faster than any player can run. After we've taken a good first touch and a shot is not available, the very next best thing is a pass that either keeps possession or sets up an attack. The first touch can also be a pass. A player will use their control of the ball and their ability to pass the most out of any of the three skills of; dribbling, passing, or shooting. This is because the pass is so effective and requires the least amount of effort to create the best goal-scoring opportunities. Players should spend most of their time learning how to pass the ball effectively, with in-game pressure.

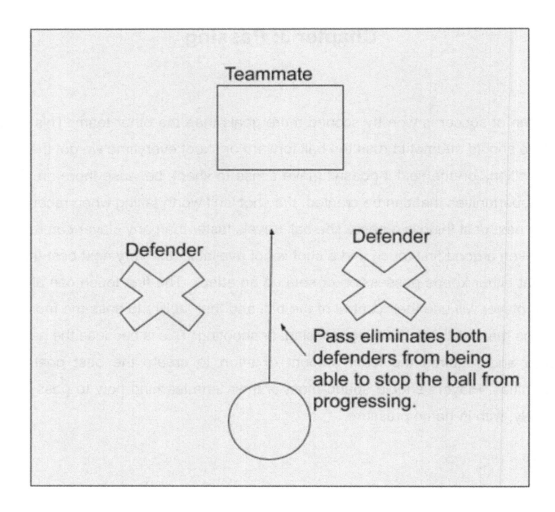

As we see in the most recent drawing, a pass can eliminate two players. This is easier to accomplish than trying to dribble past two defenders. Dribbling should only be used to create a pass or shot when there isn't a better pass or shot available.

There are several ways to pass a ball. The most common occurring pass in soccer ranges from 5-15 yards. This is where players should spend most of their time training their ability to pass effectively. For passing at this distance, it is best to use the inside of the foot closer to the ankle while making contact with the middle of the ball, maintaining a soccer posture.

The reasons for using the inside of the foot closer to the ankle; it has the greatest surface area to strike the ball making less room for error, and it allows the foot to remain stable when a player strikes the ball. If you strike the ball with the inside of the foot by the toes, you'll notice you have less control and less power because by the inside of the foot by toes the ankle is less able to keep the foot stable. The part of the foot you would use to make an effective 5-15 yard pass is the same part of the foot that is most effective for receiving a pass. When watching a professional game, try to notice how players use the inside of the foot to be able to pass and control the ball.

To train this aspect of soccer it is best to repeat the same movement of connecting the pass against a wall or to a teammate while focusing on a several mechanics of the pass working together; having good soccer posture, making sure the foot that is planted is pointing to where the pass is going, swinging the leg while the toes point up and using the inside of the foot closest to the ankle while following through.

*I do not own the image above. This image is used for educational purposes only.

To consistently have well-struck passes, it is important to stare at the part of the ball you're going to strike as your foot makes contact with the ball. When a player is training their passing ability it is easy for them to fall into a lull where they aren't actively focusing on all the details involved in making sure every pass is perfect. When this occurs, the quality of the pass becomes subpar. A golden nugget that is important to understand when training or practicing anything is understanding the principle of congruence. The principle of congruence is the idea that the way an individual does one thing is how they do everything. If a player is training inside of a lull where they aren't mentally engaged, their progress is slower and less cemented into their second nature. The way you train and the way you play are congruent. If you train incorrectly, you are going to have bad performances.

The next type of pass a player should master is a 25-30 yard driven pass. The 25-30 yard pass is different than the inside of the foot pass because it uses the laces rather than the inside of the foot. The inside of the foot pass produces less power because the muscles on the inside of the leg, closest to the centerline of a person, aren't as strong as the quadriceps muscles. Using the laces allows the body to use the quadriceps, which generates more power when striking the ball. The best part of the laces to use is; the top of the foot, the hardest part of the foot. To drill this technique, use a wall or partner and repeat the 25-30 yard driven pass technique until the pass is second nature.

The last technique is the chipped pass. The chip pass is a tough skill to master as it involves passing the ball in the air and trying to land it in an advantageous position for a teammate, which requires a lot of skill. When attempting to connect a chipped pass in a game, it is important to make sure that a chipped pass is required in the given scenario. There are many times when a player will use a chipped pass when the best way to connect the pass was to keep the ball on the floor. The criteria for making sure a chipped pass is necessary are; a teammate is open behind a defender that is blocking the direct path of the pass, or if the teammate is 40-50 yards away. If one of these two criteria are met it is often the best choice to play the ball in the air so it is not blocked by a defender or slowed down by the friction of the floor. To chip a pass a player must use the laces in the same way they would drive a pass but focus on placing their foot where the ball meets the floor and swing underneath while directing the ball forward and upward.

In the picture above we can see the legendary Andrea Pirlo using his laces as he is about to wedge his foot where the ball meets the floor, and send the ball in the air to a teammate. Notice that the leg which is going to make contact with the ball, is turned in slightly to expose the laces and make using the laces more available. The biggest errors that occur when trying to chip a pass are; not getting the foot underneath the ball enough, not pushing the ball far enough away from the body,, leaning too far to either side of the body, or not keeping the ankle stable while striking the ball. Keep in mind as you train this technique to still stare at where you're going to make contact on the ball, and make sure you're driving your foot as a wedge between the ball and the floor. To hit the ball further you can follow through, or if you want to make it shorter, stop the foot as it makes contact with the ball. To train this technique you can start off close to a goal and work on the strike repeatedly by hitting it into an empty net or wall while focusing on the contact. As you get better, try to chip the ball to a teammate at a further distance or use several soccer balls to chip at an empty net from further away. Repetition is the mother of all skills. What can happen after a handful of unsuccessful repetitions is that the player begins to get frustrated, and as the frustration grows, so does the number of unsuccessful repetitions. When drilling a new skill remain level headed by evaluating each repetition, think about what you can do to make an improvement, whether it is a slight adjustment, or completely changing one element of the technique to better fit your body.

When a player receives the ball and can't make an effective shot, the next best option is to look for a pass that either retains possession or sets up an attack. There are 3 fundamental ways to pass the ball, each having their own criteria allowing a player to understand which passing technique should be used. The highest percentage pass for finding a teammate is the 5-20 yard pass on the floor. To connect a pass 25-30 yards away use the driven pass technique. To play the ball into an advantageous position for a teammate that is 40-50 yards away, or if your teammate has space but is behind a defender, use the chipping technique to connect the pass. The mechanics of the pass are the foundation of having an effective strike on the ball.

Mechanics of a pass:
- Having good soccer posture,
- Leaning forward and not leaning too much to one side
- Making sure the foot that is planted is pointing to where the pass is going.
- Take a step towards the ball.
- Swinging the leg while the toes either point up or down depending on which technique is being used.
- Using the inside of the foot closest to the ankle of the striking foot while following through for an inside the foot pass.
- Using the laces at the center of the ball for a driven pass.
- Using the laces where the ball meets the floor, and wedging the foot under and upward for a chipped pass.

To make the best use out of time and effort, it is best to use a wall to practice inside of the foot pass or driven passes. To practice a chipped pass a player should use an open goal at a close enough distance to see the ball have backspin at a decent height and progress into using a teammate at a 30-40 yard distance or using several soccer balls and trying to chip them into a goal from 30-40 yards away.

The pass is nothing without a useful first touch. If the first touch is bad, the rest of the time in possession is most likely going to be wasted. Work on both the first touch and different types of passing simultaneously with a wall or teammate. As a player works on these techniques it is important they consistently evaluate each repetition and determine why the repetition failed or was successful.

Chapter 4: You miss 100% of the shots you do not shoot.....on frame

The trick with scoring a lot of goals is to make sure you are in prime scoring positions and focusing on getting as many high percentage shots off as possible. If you put yourself in a good position 90% of the work is done; the other 10% is shooting technique. This chapter will cover both of these elements.

To score more goals you have to understand where most goals occur and how to get in these positions as frequently as possible. Most goals are scored in the penalty box. It seems like an easy observation, but most attacking players do not get in the box enough, or waste opportunities trying to shoot from too far away. Lesson one on scoring more goals is to get the ball in the box whether on the dribble or from a pass. The next drawing shows the best place to be for scoring opportunities.

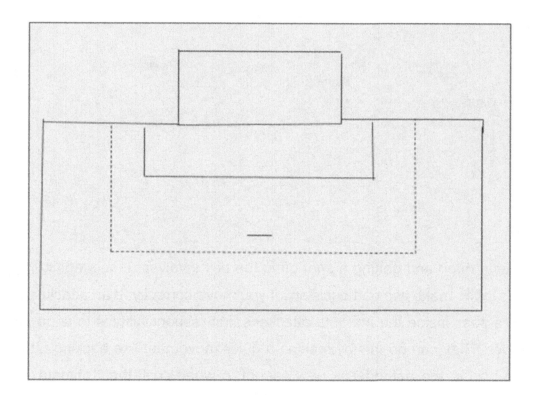

Inside the dotted rectangle is where most goals are scored for a couple of reasons; you're in front of the goal making the angle to score in either corner more available, you're close enough where any shot's power is amplified by how close it is to the goal, and the goalie's ability to react is tested tremendously because they have less time to see and deal with the shot. Here's the issue; no team is going to just let you have space in the box to shoot. This makes movement off the ball, knowing where to be, and being able to know what comes next that much more important. If we look at modern-day goal scorers they are able to create space with movement and make a defender's job miserable.

Idea 1:

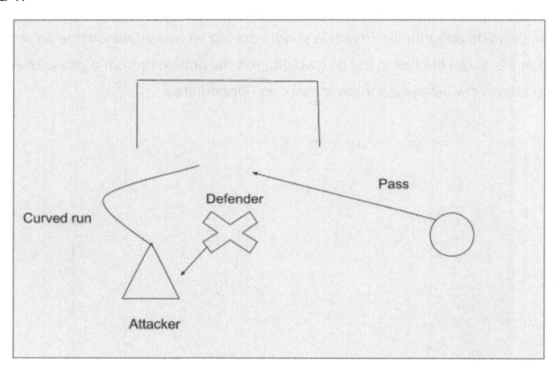

Getting open and getting a shot off in the box involves understanding how the defender is left to make two bad decisions if you move correctly. If an attacker is trying to receive a pass inside the box, the attacker's first responsibility is to separate from the defender. They can do this by making a quick movement like backing up quickly. When this occurs the defender is now caught in what I call the "Ultimate Tomato" named by The Titans, the youth team I coach. The Ultimate Tomato's name was originally the "Ultimate Ultimatum", meaning giving the defender two bad decisions to choose from, and using whatever they decide against them. In idea 1, once the attacker makes the quick movement of backing up and distances themselves from the defender, the defender has to either block the run or close the space stepping close to the attacker. When the defender chooses poorly, the attacker should respond by going where there is more space. Here's a golden nugget: the more time and space an attacker or player in possession has, the easier it is to play. By attacking where there is more space in the box and receiving the ball, the attacker's ability to generate a goal-scoring shot is amplified.

Idea 1 presented with a pass down from the middle of the field

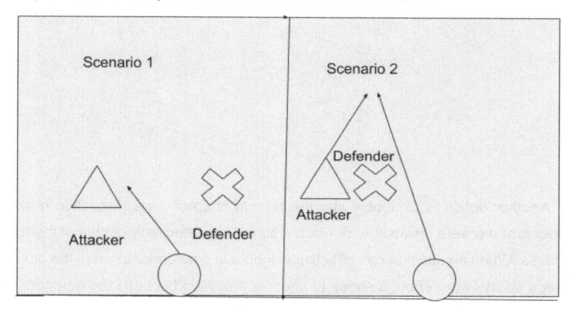

Once the forward has made a quick movement to create space from the defender, the defender will most likely choose one of the two depicted scenarios above. In either case, the forward has now found themselves with the ball in space, again the more time and space the easier it is to play. A player can drill this technique by starting next to a cone and as a teammate looks for a pass they separate from the cone and attack space either behind or in front of the cone. I recommend training to receive a pass both behind and in front of the cone because both are likely to happen when getting the ball in the box.

Idea 2 for getting a shot off in the box

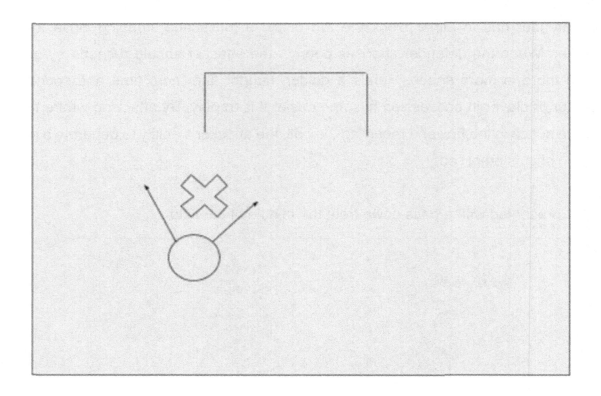

Another option is to dribble into the box. In chapter 1 we discussed how the defender is at a severe disadvantage when a player can effectively dribble at them and use moves. When an attacker can effectively dribble at a defender close to the box, the attacker's ability to get enough space to shoot is amplified because the defender has to be extremely cautious they don't cause a foul inside the box. An attacker's ability to get past a defender is also enhanced if the defender is placed in a situation where they have to choose quickly to either block a shot, or stop a dribbler. If the dribbler mixes in some deception, like a pump fake and change of direction, more often than not, the defender will try to block the fake shot. Once a move creates separation from the defender, the player in possession now has enough space to get a shot off effectively.

Once the attacker receives a pass with enough space to shoot, positioning the ball for the best possible shot becomes critical. For example, if the ball is too close to a player's centerline or is caught underneath the attacker, the attacker's ability to generate an accurate shot with force will be compromised.

The most common reason for missed shots is poor shooting alignment. To shoot effectively, the ball has to line up with one leg. The issues that players face when trying to line up a shot are; the ball is too close to their centerline, the ball is too far laterally from their centerline, or the ball is behind their hips as they go to strike the ball. When the ball is in proper alignment, shooting a goal scoring shot is significantly easier. To make sure the shot is aligned, I use the principle I call "45 degrees."

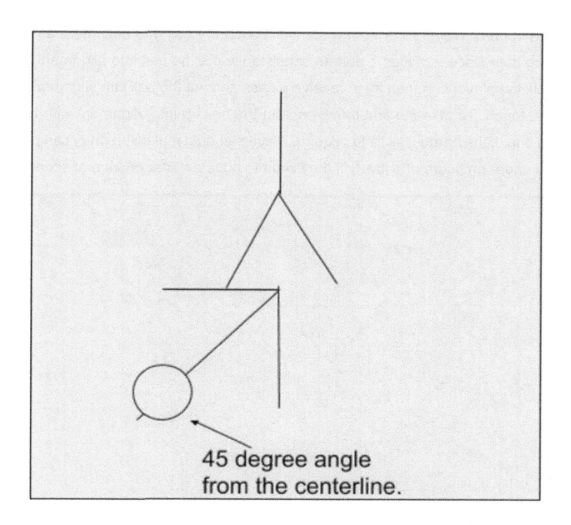

45 degree angle
from the centerline.

To avoid the common issues of positioning the ball too far laterally or too centered, we cut both of these issues in half using the 45-degree angle when pushing the ball forward or approaching the ball. This puts us in alignment to shoot effectively and makes the rest of the mechanics of shooting more fluid. The first touch can minimize the time the defender has to block the ball when the first touch sets up the shot using the 45-degrees principle. A major contributor for the defender's ability to stop a shot is usually the player in possession not having enough time and space because the first touch was bad and they have to waste time just getting the shot into alignment. Once a player finds himself with the ball in a goalscoring position, the quicker they can get their body to align with the ball the better, no matter if it is off the dribble, a first-time shot, or taking a touch and shooting.

To practice the skill of making sure the ball is in alignment a player can start off behind a cone or player, and from a standstill push the ball into alignment and try to shoot the ball. Once a player is able to consistently put the ball into alignment from a standstill, the player can then try to receive a pass and put the ball into alignment using their first touch. To take the first touch and set the ball up into alignment with the first touch is one of the hardest skills to acquire. Players should make sure they can perform this skill under pressure effectively if they want to have a better chance of scoring.

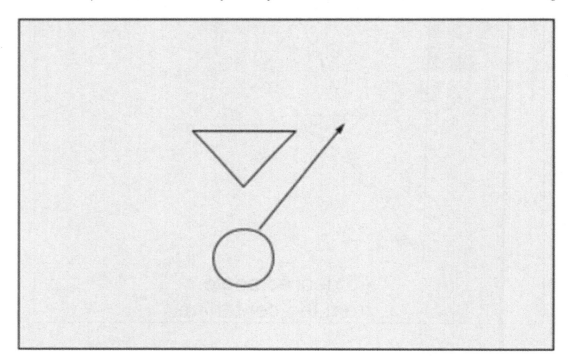

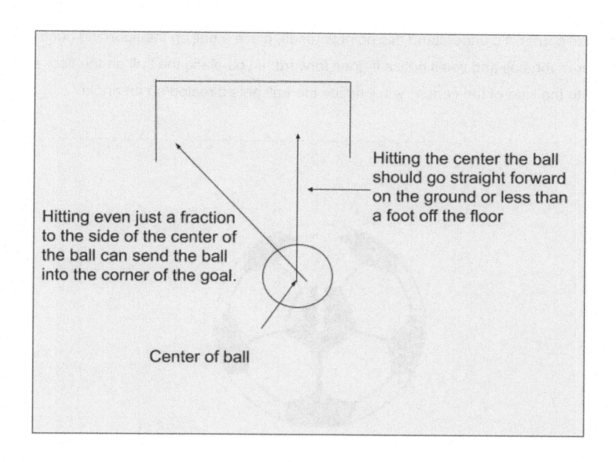

Hitting even just a fraction to the side of the center of the ball can send the ball into the corner of the goal.

Hitting the center the ball should go straight forward on the ground or less than a foot off the floor

Center of ball

Had I known about this next aspect of shooting sooner, I would have scored many more goals, and I hope whoever reads this, implements this concept whenever they are shooting. When I was playing youth soccer and even in High school, I use to dribble around multiple defenders and get in range to score, and then completely shank what should have been a definite goal. I finally realized what I was doing wrong. I was looking at the goal and just swinging my leg at the ball. As a player shoots, it is important to stare at the ball and reference the center of the ball throughout the entirety of their shot. Looking at the goal before shooting is okay for making sure you know where you want to shoot the ball, but once a player knows where they want to shoot the ball, they should only stare at the ball.

Here's another golden nugget; use the center of the ball as a reference point.

When a player is able to shoot the ball straight forward consistently this means they are able to identify the center of the ball and place a strike on it to send it forward. This also means that the same player is only a fraction off if they want to send the ball into the corner. To understand this point yourself, place a ball on the floor and push the center of the ball and you'll notice it goes forward. If you place the ball on the floor and push to the side of the center, you'll notice the ball gets directed on an angle.

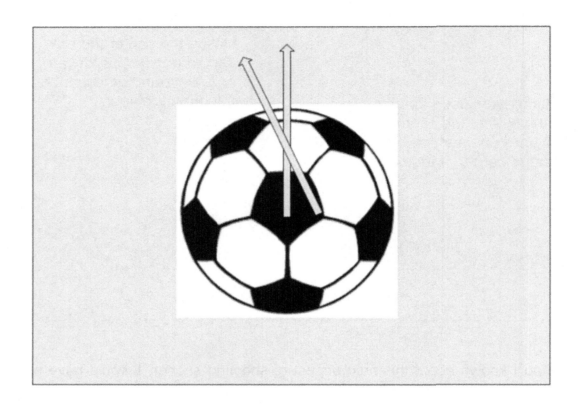

Using the center of the ball as a reference point is like having a cheat sheet to stare at while you are taking an exam. It completely takes the guesswork out of the shot and makes shooting quicker. The more drastic the angle, the further from the center of the ball the player will have to go if they want to find the corner of the goal.

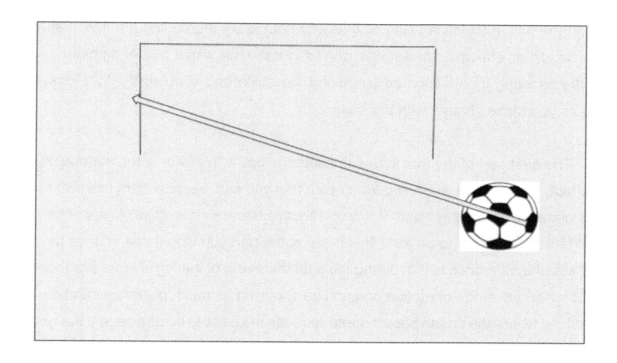

Now that we understand alignment and foot placement to create an effective shot, the next element to look at for shooting is the swing of the foot and the body mechanics involved in creating power. The swing of the leg is where the power of the shot comes from. When a player can't strike the ball with power, it is not because they aren't strong enough, it is usually because they do not swing their leg through its full range of motion. In games, a player can tense up and reduce the power of their shot by also reducing the range of motion of their swing. A player has used their full range of motion in their swing when they have drawn the leg back as far as they can while keeping balance and swung their foot forward enough to where the planted foot has come off the floor, and the player shooting then lands on the shooting foot.

As the swing of the leg is taking place, the foot that is shooting should be preparing to make contact with the ball. A mistake that often happens is when the player has the alignment of the shot down, the swing of the leg down, and is in enough time and space to score, but when it comes time to shoot, their ankle is loose and the shot is wasted. To elaborate when a person is using a hammer to hit a nail, the effectiveness of the hammer is not just the swing of the hammer, it is effective because the head of the hammer is secured to the wood making the power of the swing translate into the

49

head of the nail. If the swing was all that was necessary then using a rubber hammer would be just as effective. In essence, don't shoot the ball with a rubber hammer, make sure the shooting foot is secured by flexing the ankle and keeping the foot locked in place as you make contact with the ball.

The best part of the foot to use to shoot the ball with power is the surface on top of the foot. You'll notice when you touch your foot you can feel how hard this part of the foot is because it is mostly bone. It is also effective because it is closer to the ankle and doesn't allow for power to be lost. This is the same part you would use to drive the ball as a pass, the difference is that during the shot the swing of the leg is more pronounced as it uses the full range of motion and can be shot with as much power as can be used accurately, where the driven pass instead requires the pass to be at a pace a teammate can control.

Now that we understand how to get open, create time and space to shoot, and how to shoot accurately with power, the next concept that is important is how to score on a goalkeeper. This is where many players can get goal fog and squander shots. I've had my fair share of days where I would light it up during shooting practice, and when the game came and there was a goalie in the net, I would get overwhelmed and just fire the ball right at the goalie. The most embarrassing example of this was for me when I was playing in front of a Coach named Rob Johnson, he was a professional player, and I really admired him for who he was and how great of a coach he was. In this particular game, I had a play where I dribbled through 4 players, but when I approached the goal to shoot I ended up mishitting it, and it rolled to the goalie. I was immediately taken out and Coach Rob came up to me and said, "What you did before the shot was child abuse, but the shot jeez, I don't know if you could've made it easier for the keeper." As I grabbed a drink and sat on the bench I remember being so upset with myself and thinking about what happened? Why couldn't I score that one? A few answers came to mind. The first being that I wasn't in that situation enough when I trained on my own or with a team, to feel confident in-game. I was shooting on an empty net without considering what it'd be like when there is a goalie in there. The next thing I realized is

50

that there's a whole game in itself just beating a keeper with a shot.

There are 4 ways to score on a goalie; shooting to either their left, right, over them, or through the legs and into the goal. There are a few ways we can increase our chances of beating the keeper. If we can identify the largest amount of space left open from the goalie and place the shot there, it will usually be a goal-scoring shot, unless the goalie makes a great save. We can also make the goalie move, and give us more space if we use deception to make the goalie block where we aren't shooting, and put the ball elsewhere. If we combine deception, and putting the ball where there is more open space in the goal, that is usually a recipe for a goal and a reason to celebrate.

There are also times where the goalkeeper's reaction time should be taken into account. For example, if the goalie has a defender in front of him who is blocking his vision, shooting past the defender and using him as a screen, makes it very hard for the goalie to see the shot coming. So as the ball is moving towards the goal, the goalie sees it later during its journey, giving the goalie less time to react and block the shot. As we talked about earlier, whenever an opponent has to solve a problem with a limited amount of time, it becomes harder to answer or unanswerable all together.

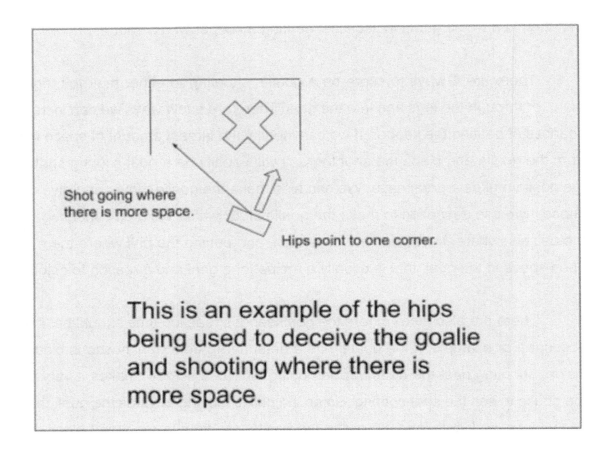

Shot going where there is more space.

Hips point to one corner.

This is an example of the hips being used to deceive the goalie and shooting where there is more space.

Understanding the elements of space, deception, giving the goalie as little time to react as possible, and shooting effectively, is what makes a player a goalscorer. Training these elements begins with a player being able to shoot effectively first. Once a player has an effective shot, they should start training with shots evolving from different in-game scenarios. For example, a player can drill receiving a through ball, taking a touch that sets up their shot, and trying to hit a corner while visualizing how a goalie would respond to the deception during the shot and the shot itself. It is one thing to just shoot on an open goal, it is another to shoot on a goal with conditions that make the shot more like an in-game scenario. Training with these ideas in mind will give players confidence when they are faced with scoring on a goalie.

It is important to consider how the goalie is shutting down angles when they come out of the goal. The closer the goalie is to the ball the less angle a player has to score. The most dangerous part for the goalie when minimizing an angle occurs as they leave the goal and haven't fully closed an angle down. As the goalie approaches the ball it makes it difficult for them to make a save as they are focusing on several things at once such as; positioning, reading the game, addressing the player with the ball, preparing to make a save, and managing the distance between themselves and the ball. As this is happening, a player who is shooting is looking for where there is more space. If a goalie gets so close there is no angle, dribble past the goalie and shoot it into an empty net.

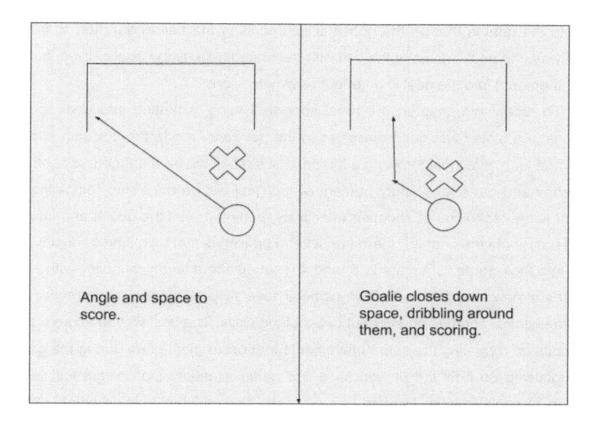

Angle and space to score.

Goalie closes down space, dribbling around them, and scoring.

A Golden nugget; "Inside the box, inside the foot.". The inside of the foot is the best option to use for a pass for 5-20 yards. Inside the box is less than 18 yards from the goal. Using the inside of the foot can make it easier to place a shot into the corner. Using the laces generates a powerful shot, but it doesn't just take power to score on a goalkeeper, it takes enough power and accuracy to put the ball past the goalie and into the goal. If you just try to blast it, you'll most likely miss the frame of the goal altogether, but if you tone down the power and focus on placing the ball where there is more space

53

in the goal, you'll always have a higher chance of scoring than missing the frame altogether. If a player can blast the ball with full force accurately that is another recipe for a goal, but all that is required to score on a goalie is enough power to put the ball past the goalie and into the goal.

Putting it to the left or right of the goalie are the most frequently used ways to score, but you can also put the ball over the goalie or through the goalie's legs. If the goalie is too far forward from the goal, there is space to put the ball above them and have it fall under the crossbar. Another reason you would put the ball over the goalie and into the goal is that as the goalie is approaching the ball in an effort to stop a breakaway, the goalie dives at the ball with their hands, so as the goalie dives, putting it over them and into the goal is an effective way to score.

To recap this chapter; the most important thing is getting into goal scoring positions. If a player can get themselves in the hot zone, inside the box with enough space and time, even just throwing a toe poke at the ball will be a dangerous shot. Get in the box and get open, ninety percent of the goal will be done; the remaining ten percent is the technique of shooting effectively, putting it past the goalie and into the goal. Throughout the chapter, there are several principles that take time for a player to adapt into their game. Chapters 2, 3, and 4 were all about technical ability with some sprinkles of how to apply the skills in-game. These skills take consistent practice and effort to acquire. There is no shortcut to acquiring skills. The best way to acquire skills is to focus on repeating the same movements that occur most often during the game, while focusing on how they'll work in a live game situation. Do not get lost in the delusion of social media. Players can get side tracked from training what is most important by trying to work on something they saw on social media. Focus on what the game requires most consistently at every level. In the next chapter, we're going to cover principles for training and some suggestions to get the most out of your training.

Chapter 5: Training Principles…. Grit X Correct training = Player growth

Chapters 2, 3, and 4 focused on the tools and skills that will be most used during a game. This chapter looks at the principles of training and how to get the most out of training sessions. In one of Abraham Lincoln's most famous quotes he states, "If you gave me six hours to cut down a tree, I'll spend the first four sharpening the ax." To get to a higher level in soccer, it is important that players understand that they have to be constantly trying to sharpen their skills and break to new levels of control and speed of play. The best way to sharpen soccer skills is consistent training, focusing on a high number of repetitions that can work in a live game scenario. When players are working on a skill that is new to them, it is important that they have a level of grit. A lot of players beginning to learn a skill that is new to them will begin to get frustrated, and want to stay away from learning the skill. When I was a youth soccer player and began learning to juggle the ball, I remember my Dad pushing me to keep working on it. I can still remember the frustration of getting two or three juggles and not being able to just get five. Sometimes I'd be outside for hours trying to juggle and go through an emotional roller coaster when I thought to myself, "Am I ever going to get 100 juggles in a row?" As I kept pushing I was able to get to higher numbers. My most recent juggling record is 10,000 juggles in a row. That record took me 2 hours to complete. Looking back at my youth soccer journey, I was always the smallest player, and I was also very slow. The reason I was able to compete at higher levels was that I had more grit than most people.

If you can combine grittiness with efficient and effective methods of training, your growth as a soccer player will skyrocket.

Training Principles

The Use/Disuse principle states what you do not use, you lose. The more a person repeats something, the more it is ingrained into their central nervous system, but the skills can be lost if they aren't practiced consistently. What happens with a lot of youth players is that they think they can just show up to practice twice a week and a game on the weekend and get better. For some players, they might develop somewhat with this routine, but their growth will be limited and they will reach a plateau sooner than later. Getting to higher levels of soccer requires consistent, daily, training and sharpening of skills. If this seems like it is a chore and something you want to shy away from that is fine, but know you'll only unlock a fraction of your soccer potential.

The Kaizen principle can be defined as the pursuit of getting better fractionally every day and having it compound. For example, trying to get 100% better in one day is impossible, but getting 1% or a fraction of one percent better each day is possible. If a player gets 1% better everyday for 3 years they will have gotten better by 1000%. It is always better to do a little rather than not doing anything at all. Every day doesn't have to be as strenuous as a game. If players feel fatigued or worn out they can still get some work in by training skills that aren't as intense. My favorite exercise for recovery days is juggling the ball. It doesn't strain your body and can be a great way to break up lactic acid inside the muscles. Get something out of every day.

The In-game principle can be defined as making sure what you are training and how you are training translates into making you a better player. It is easy to go outside and just shoot the ball at an open net and then waste time retrieving the ball. Shooting is certainly important, but make sure your training is making you a better player. For example, if a player wants to get better at passing, and they already have a decent technical ability to pass, their training should focus on how well they can pass with different types of pressure. Can they connect a pass with a defender running at them? Can they make space as the defender runs at them by making a move and then connect a pass? By adding game elements to the training, you'll be better prepared for the game. If you're not on the ball, that doesn't mean you can't still make leaps in your understanding of the game. A player can still get better without the ball if they can visualize as vividly as possible how well the skills will work and the different types of reactions a defender will have.

As a player gets better it is very important they try to perform their skills at faster speeds. The game gets faster as you get to higher levels. Playing at faster speeds requires players to be able to solve situations faster, which forces the commands from the brain to the feet to be faster. The only way that the command from the brain to the feet is fast enough is if you train to complete commands as fast as you can. There will be times where you have time and space on the field and it doesn't require you to play as fast as possible, but if you have the ability to play fast, as a byproduct, you'll always have the ability to play slower. First get the mechanics down, second be able to perform them with pressure, and then work on how fast you can perform the skills while focusing on how fast you can solve situations that may arise in the game.

The adaptation principle is the idea that the body is very resilient and will always look to adapt to whatever is going on. For example, if someone lifts weights the body breaks down muscle tissue and builds it back stronger to compensate for the demand that was previously placed on the body. This same principle can be applied to acquiring skills. Let's say a player can't box the ball at first, but they keep focusing on what they want it to look like when they get better; As the player keeps trying to match their current ability with how they want the skill to be performed, it is forcing the body to adapt and eventually be able to produce the skills. As I said earlier, this process of acquiring, sharpening, and maintaining skills is a constant grind. It takes a lot of grit to get to higher levels of skill, you have to first love what you're doing and then attack what you're trying to obtain repeatedly until you feel confident in performing the skill in-game under pressure. Force your mind and body to adapt to what you want to be able to do.

Chapter 6A: "Football is played with the head. Your feet are just tools." - Andrea Pirlo

Soccer IQ can be defined as a player's understanding of how to solve situations on the field. The ability for a player to resolve a play on the field and have their solution translate into a goal-scoring play, is what the players at the highest levels get paid to do. Professional players get paid not because they can run fast, shoot, or dribble past everyone. Professional players get paid because they are able to use the skill set they have, to solve problems that lead to their team to scoring more goals than the other team. If you look at most professional teams, you'll notice players come in all different sizes. If we look at FC Barcelona for the last couple of years you'll see players over six foot and other players around five foot six. FC Barcelona is amongst one of the best clubs in Europe and can afford to bring in the very best players from around the world. Why would FC Barcelona choose a player who is short and not the strongest, when they could bring in the biggest, fastest, most expensive players in the world? The reason they would pick players who may be shorter and slower is that those players are able to resolve plays on the field in their positions better, and faster than other players. It is easier to train an athlete to run faster or get stronger than it is to teach them to play the game better. My aim for this chapter is to provide ideas and inspiration for how to look at the game and help you play soccer better.

The Time-Space continuum

The time-space continuum is a foundational concept that should be part of everyone's training. The time-space continuum is the understanding of the space a player has around them and what works inside that space. There are several different ways to be aware of space or to create space. Before we get into those concepts, it is important players begin with the proper context in mind. The more time and space a player has, the easier it is to play. If you've ever gone to an open soccer field alone with a ball and tried to score it was probably very easy, not because of your skillset, but because you had so much time and space you could dribble the ball into the goal while walking if you wanted. When we step into a game, we have a lot less time and space, but we can make the best use out of that time and space to allow us to use our skills effectively. Going forward in this chapter, remember the more time and space, the better. There are times where separating from a defender isn't an option, but even with a defender nearby, a player can still create time and space. Let's get into it.

The first way to get the ball in a pocket of space is to have purposeful movement off the ball. It is always harder to defend someone, with or without the ball, if they are moving. It requires more effort to defend someone who is constantly moving, especially if the player on offense is thinking a couple of moves ahead of the defender.

When a player has found themselves in space, the next thing they have to do is position themselves so they can receive the ball in a way that sets up their next move. For example, if a player is running to get open and receives the ball with their back to the field, they will waste time and space adjusting, and will be closed down before they can make their move.

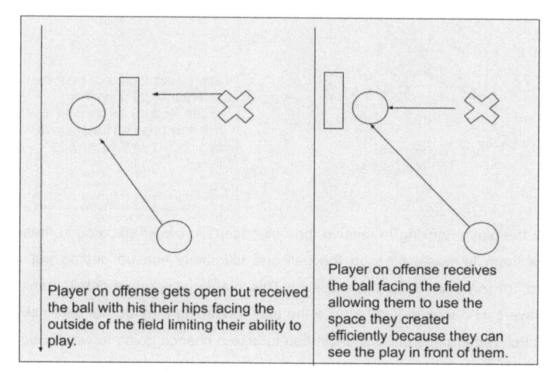

Player on offense gets open but received the ball with his their hips facing the outside of the field limiting their ability to play.

Player on offense receives the ball facing the field allowing them to use the space they created efficiently because they can see the play in front of them.

In the drawing above, we can see the player receives the ball and that their back is facing away from the field while the defender is closing them down. This limits their ability to play because they can't see what is behind them, and as they try to figure out what is around them the defender can begin applying pressure and taking away time and space from the player that moved. Time and space are limited; choosing the most advantageous body position will relieve the pressure created by the opposing player.

This concept can be applied when there are multiple defenders around as well. For example, let's say we have a central midfielder who is looking to receive the ball from an outside defender. As that player looks to get open, it becomes even more important that they set themselves up for success for when they get the ball because there is a lot more pressure in the center of the field.

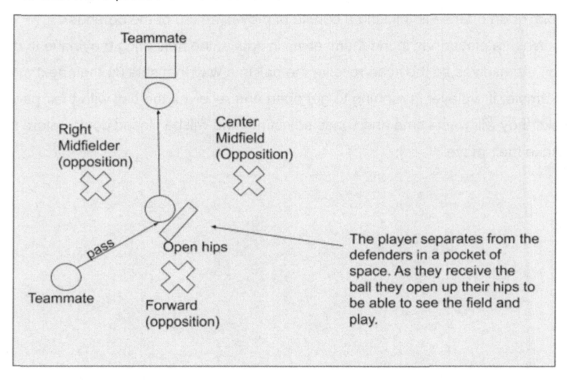

If the player looking to receive the ball doesn't know what's around them, it is easy for them to waste time on the ball and ultimately end up getting put under pressure, forcing them to lose possession. This is a very important detail; there are a lot of players who look to just "survive the play", meaning they do not take risks and would much rather pass the ball back than to take a chance going forward. Soccer is not won by who can just survive. Soccer is won by who can create chances and score, while limiting the other team's chances. If all you're doing is surviving the play then you will never create chances. To have fun while playing soccer, you have to be adventurous and take chances, whether that is taking a player on, or trying to find a through ball to a teammate, or even just shooting. Do not be scared to lose the ball in an attempt to create a chance. Understand that if you are getting open and setting yourself up to play, you're already in a better position to complete the adventurous play, not to mention that if you've sharpened up your skills and are confident, you're better off going at the other team with everything you've got and enjoying it.

How do we determine what space to run into, and how to set ourselves up to receive the ball? The best answer to that is to first look at what is around you. If you know there is a defender coming on your right and you can receive the ball on your left then that is already playing one step ahead. If we can see where we are going to pass to next, before we even get the ball, then we can take the first touch away from the defender, setting up the pass to our teammate. The first layer is awareness. A common mistake a player can make as they are looking for space is to take one long stare and try to play off what they saw while only seeing the field for that limited time. It is always better to take quick snapshots of the ball and then what is around you as you play. Looking before you receive the ball with quick glances is the foundation of the time-space continuum. Inside the time-space continuum is the principle called "know before you go." The know before you go principle states you must know what is around you and the situation you're going to create, before you run to get open. If you do not know what is around and what you are creating with your movement, then you are just running for the sake of running.

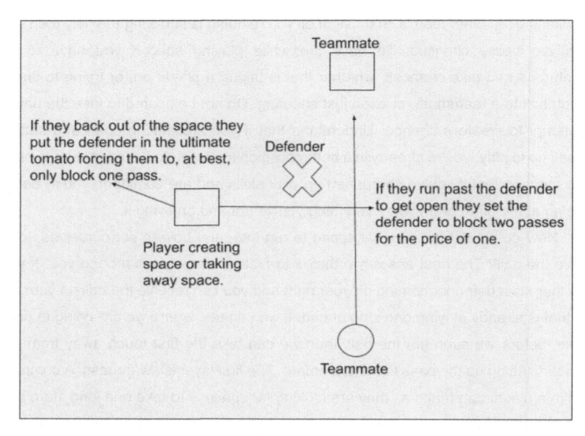

Teammate

If they back out of the space they put the defender in the ultimate tomato forcing them to, at best, only block one pass.

Defender

If they run past the defender to get open they set the defender to block two passes for the price of one.

Player creating space or taking away space.

Teammate

The movement off the ball has to be purposeful. To make sure that the movement is purposeful, a player must be able to glance and see what is around them and understand what their movement is setting up. In the drawing above we can see that the player who is either creating space or reducing the amount of space, can have a huge impact on the play even without getting the ball. By running in front of the defender they close down the passing lane to their teammate, but if they back away from the space they can create two passing lanes and almost eliminate the defender all together. That right there is what soccer is all about. If a player can recognize these types of situations, know what is around them, know where they are going to next, and have the skills to be able to execute it all, who can stop them? Nobody.

Once we understand "know before you go", the space around you, and setting up the next play, players should look for what is the best possible decision. Possession is a very important factor for soccer. If your team has the ball, the other team can't score; but does that mean teams should focus on possessing more than trying to break through the other team's defense? If it is possible to break through the other team's defense with one pass why wouldn't you? A player can find themselves in a situation where they have an easy pass readily available while also having the money pass that breaks through the other team's defense. How do they know which one to choose? This is where the topic of intentionality comes into play. Intentionality is the process of quickly deciding which option will be the most threatening to the opposing team.

Playing with intention is what separates a lot of players from being an average player to being a top player at any level. When you're watching a game try to look for players who look like everything they do on the field is to beat the other team. A player who is a great example of this is Suarez on FC Barcelona. Suarez has great skills and athletic ability, but what makes him the center forward on one of the best teams in the world, is his hunger and his intentions on the field. He will do whatever it takes to make sure he gets to shoot and score, whether it is dribbling past defenders, getting on the end of crosses, or getting open in the box to get a shot off. His entire game revolves around getting the ball in the net by any means. It is easy to try and simply survive the play by doing the safe pass. The safe pass is always available whether it is turning and playing the ball back to a teammate, or giving the ball to a teammate in close proximity. Playing just trying to keep the ball and not make any mistakes is the scourge of soccer development. Whenever a parent or coach sees a player make a mistake the first emotional response is to holler at the player and try to correct what they did wrong. This makes a lot of players more worried about not messing up and forces them to want the safer option more than taking the risk of creating a play that has more rewards.

If a player is focusing more on not messing up rather than playing with intentions to win, their playing ability is severely diminished because they are playing without purpose. Soccer is won by scoring more goals than the other team. You can not beat the other team by surviving the play. You have to play with intentions of attacking the other team and scoring. One of my favorite players ever, named Filippo Inzaghi, was a skinny, slow, and mediocre skilled player, but he won pretty much everything possible at the highest level of soccer. What made the difference is that he didn't care about losing the ball and certainly was not scared of messing up. At times it was questionable if he even understood the offsides rule because he was offsides so often that the referee wouldn't have the audacity to call ten offsides on the same player in one game.

He would score goals consistently through pure intentionality. He wanted that ball, and he wanted to score so bad that the context of the situation did not matter; making choosing the correct decision simple. It would come down to; does the current situation lead to a goal, if not fine, keep it safe and keep possession, but if it can lead to a goal with a dribble, pass, or shot, it'd be a mistake to not attack the other team's goal with whatever ability you have in your arsenal. It is a lot easier to make decisions when you have a set of principles in mind. When training it is important to focus on the principles listed in the book, but even more important to think of the game in your own terms, and develop your own principles. Principles take the guesswork out of decision making and help you align yourself with what it is you are trying to accomplish. They also give you a quick reference for what to think and concentrate on during the game. For example, when you are playing defense a basic principle is trying to keep the attacker away from the center of the field and keep them in front of you. This principle gives players a quick reference for where to be on the field and how to defend. That is how principles should be used, as quick references that can make the decision-making process faster and easier to process while playing. If your technical ability is at a decent level and you have fast decision making that is still a big step toward success.

During the game, if we have to receive the ball with a defender who is applying a lot of pressure to us and almost reducing the amount of space to zero, we can still manage to salvage the situation and turn it into something awesome. Remember the three-point system? That is the secret to having time and space even with a defender right on you. A defender can apply pressure and temporarily make it harder to go with the ball, but if they can't touch the ball and you can still maintain control of it while you're playing, then the defender is only making it a little more complicated to play, and there are plenty of ways to play out of it.

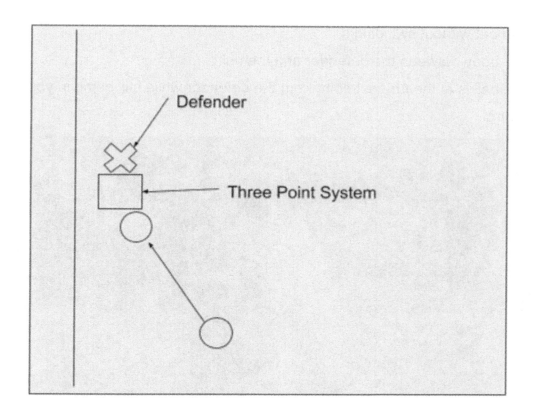

As we look at this drawing we can see that if we use our body as a roadblock for the defender between them and the ball, there is nothing they can do other than foul to get to the ball. This gives us time on the ball while taking on pressure from a defender. From this position, we can also use a series of fakes to off-balance the defender and turn or we can lay the ball off to a teammate who can begin playing with the play in front of them. If you have two defenders on you that still is not a reason to lose the ball, because that means there is an open space somewhere on the field and you should be able to think ahead and find a teammate who is available to receive the ball. When applied properly, this concept makes a dramatic impact on a player's and team's ability to keep possession and not lose the ball cheaply. When training and playing, do not shy away from playing with a defender right on you, because that is a perfect opportunity to work on, and experiment with the three-point system and harness its power. Time and space are always better to play in, but there are going to be a lot of times where you will need to use the three-point system.

- Arm out without swinging it
- The body between the defender and the ball
- The ball is at the furthest point from the defender while still being in your control

In this picture, notice how the defender has no option, but to pull and foul his way towards the ball. If you are doing it correctly, it should be hard for the defender to even see where the ball really is, making whatever move you throw at them even more believable because they have no other choice than to defend or try to block where they think the ball is going. I still haven't found an effective response to the three-point system. I'll update the book if I do, but for now, master this skill along with purposeful off the ball movement and you will be a great player with and without space.

Chapter 6B Examples of Soccer IQ being Expressed Visually

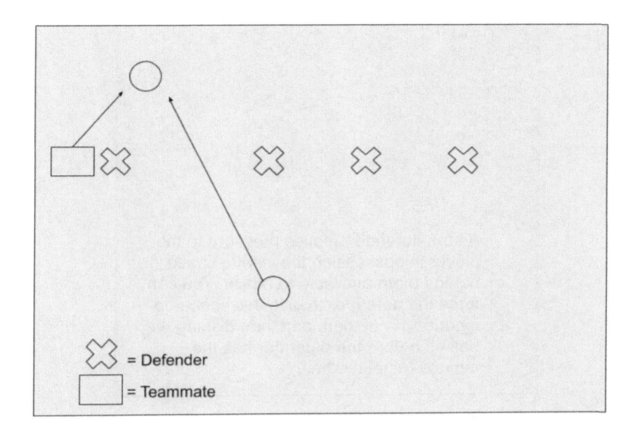

Example 1: Finding the right pass

    This represents an understanding of finding the right pass. If the player in possession of the ball tries to find their teammate right to their feet, the pass will be intercepted. The same pass, if played to the space behind the defender and in front of the teammate, is the right pass. This pass breaks a line of defense and sets the teammate up to be able to take the ball in stride and create an opportunity to score.

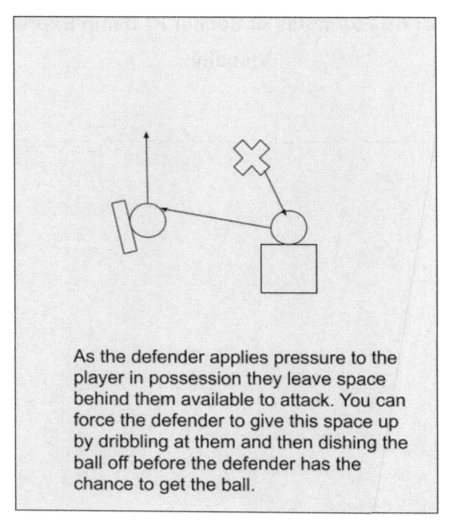

As the defender applies pressure to the player in possession they leave space behind them available to attack. You can force the defender to give this space up by dribbling at them and then dishing the ball off before the defender has the chance to get the ball.

Example 2: Explore the space

When the player in possession has the ball with a defender in front of them, they can draw the defender in by advancing towards the defender forcing the defender to address the immediate threat of the ball, leaving the space behind them available. This is an important concept to understand because as players get to higher levels, the ability to get in behind becomes more of an obstacle. Being able to recognize the space quickly and execute a pass that gets in behind is an important ability that distinguishes many players. Whether it is drawing in the defender, or playing the pass into space, it is important to practice recognizing the play that gets in behind and finding the solution that gets there.

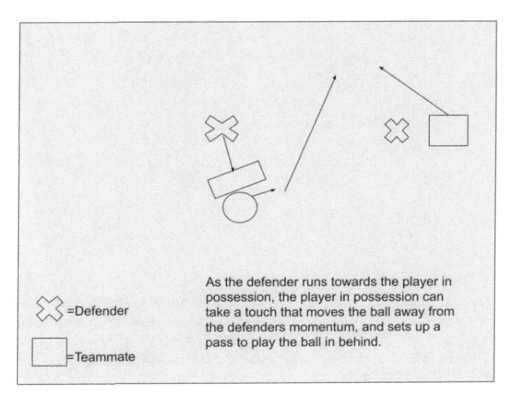

As the defender runs towards the player in possession, the player in possession can take a touch that moves the ball away from the defenders momentum, and sets up a pass to play the ball in behind.

⟨⟩ =Defender

☐ =Teammate

Example 3: Use the opponent's momentum against them

There are a series of things that need to happen before receiving the ball if you want to make the most out of the time and space you've created or found yourself in. The first thing you have to know is what is around you and be able to know where there will be defensive pressure, along with what options are available. In Example 3 you can see a defender stepping to the ball and applying pressure to the player receiving the ball. As the defender applies pressure, the player receiving the ball should know where the defender is coming from, and take a first touch that puts the ball away from the defender, giving the player in possession more time. The first touch makes time, and if possible sets up the next series of events. In Example 3, we can see that the first touch also sets up the pass. The defender has just spent energy trying to address the ball meanwhile their effort was wasted because they have to now recover back towards goal as the ball was played in behind within two touches. When a player or team can play like this it is very hard for the other team to keep up, as they waste effort, get tired, and ultimately give up after conceding. Once you've worn out the opponent, their ability to defend is diminished.

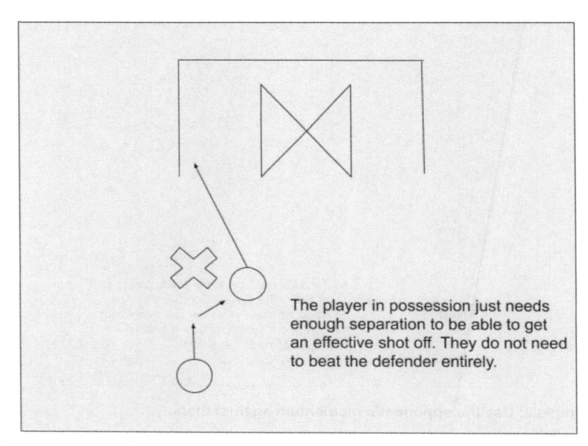

The player in possession just needs enough separation to be able to get an effective shot off. They do not need to beat the defender entirely.

Example 4: How are you going to react?

When dribbling at a defender and looking to get a shot off you can make it very difficult for the defender to stop the shot if you can make them hesitate while you quickly push the ball into space and transition into a shot. If you apply a basic move like a body feint and push the bull into a pocket of space to shoot, and hit it before the defender can come up with the defensive solution to the shot, there is no way they can block it. As a player is training they should focus on how quick they can hit a move and transition to a shot on goal. If you do this fast enough there isn't a defender who can stop the shot unless they overcompensate, priming them for the pump fake, and giving you an even better shot. The dribble that sets up the shot, and the shot itself mean nothing unless it can create a goal-scoring chance. To get the most out of your shot on goal; try to identify where you want to shoot before even setting up the shot, hit the move that allows you to separate from the defender, and then strike the ball toward where you think you would have the best chance of scoring.

Deception is Key

When in possession of the ball you can dribble, shoot, or pass while attacking directly. This is a basic level of attack and allows the defender to read the play as it is evolving. By creating misdirection with your play and not allowing the defender to be able to read your real intentions, you can create more time and space, allowing for better scoring opportunities. This can take place in the form of a pump fake, or simply opening up the hips and making it look like you're going to pass the ball elsewhere, and then find your initial target. By using misdirection, it forces the defender to either hesitate a little, or removes them from the play entirely, giving the player in possession more time. As players get to higher levels there is less time and space which forces players to assimilate by creating more time and space. If the defender can't read the real intentions of the attacker they are left to just guess, giving the attacker more of an advantage. If you have the ability to recognize the correct play and can mask your intentions, you will have a higher chance of success.

Chapter 6 summary

- Being able to apply soccer IQ comes from having a proficient technical foundation.

- Developing speed of play comes from knowing what is around you defensively and offensively.

- Using your first touch to set up your next move and make it harder for the defender to get to the ball.

- Playing with intentionality and doing the play that creates chances to score, when it is on and keeping possession when it isn't.

To conclude, this chapter I want to state these are ideas and principles that have to be molded and adapted into each individual player's style of playing. This takes a lot of effort, as well as the ability to know when a mistake was made and how to make yourself better for the next time you find yourself in that scenario. Try to keep these ideas and principles in mind and apply them to your game when at practice or in-game. These ideas work in any position, and this will give you the ability to make leaps of progress in your game.

Chapter 7: You have to get the ball first

The players in soccer who usually receive the most recognition are the goalscorers, but the players who make a difference for the majority of the game are the ones who can keep the ball out of the net and create attacks. Defending is a set of skills players do not focus on enough individually. This chapter is going to focus on skills and concepts that will improve a player's understanding of how to defend, and the principles that will help players win the ball more consistently.

The first concept that gives players a sense of what to do on defense is; making the player in possession more predictable and guiding them either backward or wide. The best way to address a player in possession of the ball is to position your body in a way that forces the player in possession into one direction.

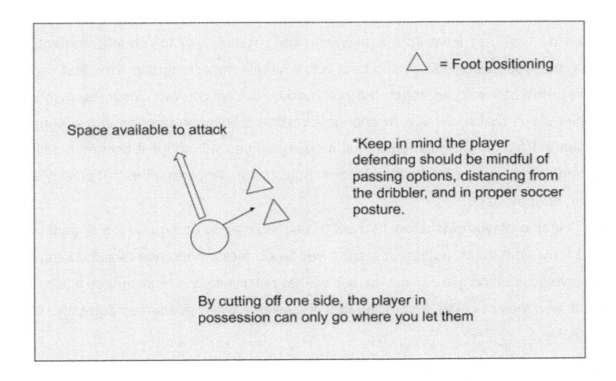

= Foot positioning

Space available to attack

*Keep in mind the player defending should be mindful of passing options, distancing from the dribbler, and in proper soccer posture.

By cutting off one side, the player in possession can only go where you let them

In the previous drawing notice the positioning of the feet and how if the player in possession goes towards the defender they are putting themselves in a position to have to fight for the ball. This makes the player in possession more likely to dribble towards the open space. Knowing that the player in possession is going to take the route you left available for them, you can make calculated, timed tackles to dispossess the player of the ball. Making the player predictable while pushing them away from the center of the field is the main priority of defending because it applies pressure to the player in possession, and forces them to have to play with what you give them, rather than have them attack your goal with several options available. Positioning yourself, knowing what is available for the player in possession to use for an attack, and making them predictable, will make the player in possession have to play technically perfect to complete the play. At the highest levels of soccer, this is what defenders get paid to do; position themselves, make players on the attack predictable, and then if possible contain or shut them down completely.

Mistakes that occur when a player is trying to use the stance defensively usually happen as they run towards the player in possession with too much momentum, making them susceptible to getting beat with a simple move to space. The best way to approach the ball is to approach the ball quickly, but as you get closer, take shorter choppier steps that allow you to change direction quickly and spring into a sprint if necessary. If you run regularly with full momentum you will notice it becomes difficult to change direction or contain the player in possession. Approach the ball quickly with shorter, choppy steps.

Once a player gets a feel for how to use the stance and guide the opponent to where they want them, putting in a solid well-timed tackle becomes easier. Using the defensive positioning ,we can set up tackles that will give us the best chance at winning the ball with less risk. The first tackle that is available when positioned correctly is the front tackle.

The defender waits until the player is
about to take a touch and then places
the outside of the foot closest to the
ball in front of the ball as a doorstop.

The player in possession has
been guided one way.

As a player puts in a front tackle, timing the tackle as the player is about to take a touch, it is important for the player putting in the tackle to have the heel of the tackling foot in the ground and try to place the outside of their ankle at the center of the ball. The reason for this is that the outside of the ankle is strong, in the sense that putting pressure directly to the outside of the ankle wouldn't rotate the foot, whereas using the area closer to where the toes are, can allow for the ball to go over the foot and have players get knocked off balance,instead of stopping the ball. The first time a player successfully jams an opponent up with this technique they will fall in love with the front tackle. There also aren't as many risks involved if the tackler can maintain their balance they have a backup plan readily available, known as the back tackle.

The back tackle can be the primary option for trying to stop an opponent who is dribbling, but if you miss the back tackle, you are surely beaten. The front tackle should be the first attempt to get the ball as it sets up the back tackle.

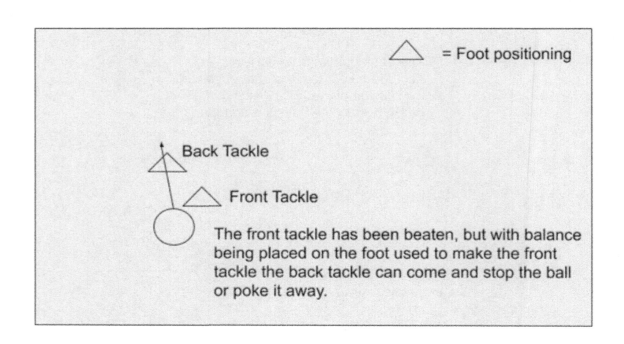

$\triangle$ = Foot positioning

Back Tackle

Front Tackle

The front tackle has been beaten, but with balance being placed on the foot used to make the front tackle the back tackle can come and stop the ball or poke it away.

Notice in the drawing above, that as the ball is moved past the front tackle, it lines up nicely for the back leg to come and clean up shop. Earlier in this book we went over how beating one leg would mean beating the whole defender, but using the defensive stance and the front and back tackles, you are forcing opponents to take on two legs making getting past you more difficult. This does require timing, and is a skill that you must work on if you want to be able to use it in games.

We have all tried to defend someone who is much faster than us, and it can be a nightmare as they turn the exchange into a foot race for the ball. How can you stop someone who is just going to knock the ball forward and take off down the line? The answer to that one is "The Wedge". This is similar to the three-point system but used in a defensive way. As you approach the ball with shorter steps and good balance you are able to change direction and react better to what the opponent is doing. When the opponent pushes the ball past you the first response is to try to wedge your body in between the ball and the player. If you stop abruptly in front of them that is a foul, but if you get in front of them and move towards the ball, even slowly, that is not a foul. This slows the faster player down and gives you the ability to take advantage of that big touch.

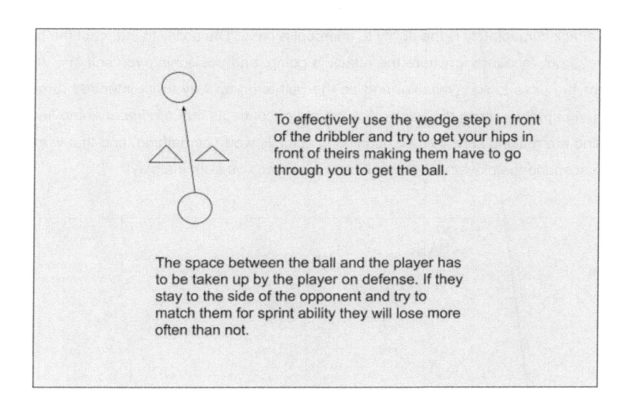

To effectively use the wedge step in front of the dribbler and try to get your hips in front of theirs making them have to go through you to get the ball.

The space between the ball and the player has to be taken up by the player on defense. If they stay to the side of the opponent and try to match them for sprint ability they will lose more often than not.

The most important part when using the wedge is obtaining an inside position between the player and the ball. Whoever dominates that space will win the ball more often than not. The wedge may not be as simple as running in front of the opponen;t they may try to shoulder you off the ball before you get that chance. The idea is to time the wedge, and if necessary shoulder tackle the opponent enough to get them off balance and then obtain inside position.

A shoulder tackle can be defined as having an arm against your body and using the side of your body, bumping into the player in possession of the ball and winning possession. It becomes a foul when the arm is extended, or the player using the tackle isn't focused on winning the ball and more focused on just slamming into the opponent. The shoulder tackle and the wedge work together to obtain the inside position. Once you have possession of the ball you can look to find a pass, or if necessary go into the three-point system to retain possession of the ball.

When playing defense, there's nothing I love better than a nice, crunching tackle, where I win the ball and completely remove the player in possession from the play, but what is a better showing of soccer intelligence and what will allow you to win the ball and attack immediately is the ability to intercept a pass. The ability to intercept the ball comes from recognizing where the attack is going, and positioning yourself in a way where the pass looks available, and as the ball is on its way to its intended target, stepping up and cutting the pass off. A couple of concepts that are important to keep in mind are making sure your positioning is actually worth something, and that worst-case scenario the player with the ball can't eliminate you from the play.

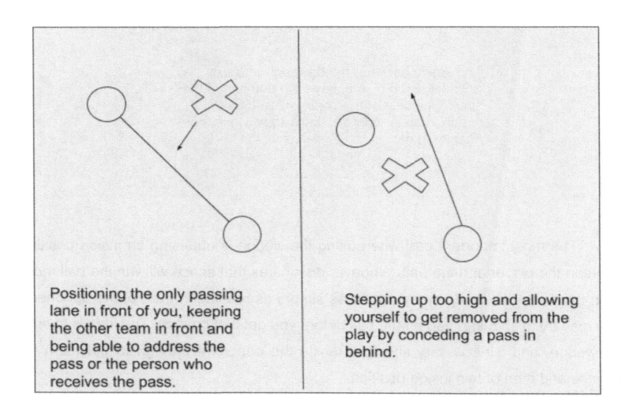

Positioning the only passing lane in front of you, keeping the other team in front and being able to address the pass or the person who receives the pass.

Stepping up too high and allowing yourself to get removed from the play by conceding a pass in behind.

By keeping the pass in front of you, and positioning yourself in a way that allows you to cut off an errant pass, or to still be able to address the player receiving the pass and go into the defensive stance and tackling system, you will make it more difficult to get beat with a pass, or on the dribble. This makes the team with the ball less likely to have an effective attack and ultimately, you and your team can win possession back and start an attack. These concepts can be applied in every position. Keep the pass in front of you, while making sure they can't play in behind.

The X represents a forward applying pressure to a team looking to build an attack in the midfield or their own defensive third.

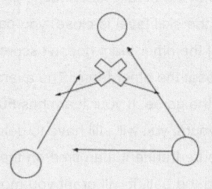

The player in possession allows the other team to have the ball in front of them while making the pass behind them harder to connect. As this is happening they can make the ball stay in front of them and force the team in possession to play laterally.

Notice how the player on Defense allows the other team to play in front of them without giving up space behind them. This is critical for not allowing the other team to progress up the field with the ball under control. Most of the time when a team is being frustrated with no options available, the team in possession will look for a long ball forward and ultimately surrender the idea of a controlled attack, and gamble to see if they can win back the long ball. At the youth level, the long ball can be found to be effective if you have a couple of players who can kick the ball high and far, and some fast forwards to run onto the long ball and shoot it at the net, but as players get to around 13 years old, that form of attack starts to become low percentage. To successfully defend a long ball it can take winning a header, controlling a loose ball, or just applying enough pressure to the player receiving the ball and forcing them to let it go by or turn it over.

Defending is a skill that begins first with keeping the play in front of you and making the team in possession predictable. Once the other team is forced to play with what is left available to them, closing down what is left becomes easier. When defending it is also very important that the other team doesn't get in behind. It doesn't matter if the other team is better if the skill level is close, you can win or compete in games by just defending properly. If the other team doesn't score they can't beat you, and then, it only takes one goal to beat the other team. The average professional has the ball less than 2% of the time in the game. If your team has 50% of the possession during the game and 2% of that is yours, you will still have to defend the other 50% of the game. This makes defending more frequent than time on the ball. Not to mention that if you are successful at winning the ball, it will grant you more time in-game with the ball.

Review of Defending

- Make the opponent predictable
- Keep the play in front of you
- Know what is available
- Know when to intercept and when to confront the player receiving the ball
- 1 on 1 defending defensive stance and foot positioning
- Front tackle
- Back tackle
- Wedge

Chapter 8: Supplemental Training

This chapter covers different ideas for how to train physically, mentally, and technically as an individual, along with some ideas on nutrition and sleep. Some of the things that held me back when I was a youth player was that I had no concept of how to train physically, and I definitely did not eat or sleep properly. It might not seem like it would make a big difference at the youth level, but eating the right foods and getting enough rest can be the difference in rates of progress.

If a player isn't eating right or getting enough sleep they are a lot more likely to get sick or injured. Time spent recovering is the same time that could be spent getting better at soccer, but instead, it is being used just to get back to where you were. I'm not saying anyone can go entirely injury-free or never get sick, but a player can reduce the rate of getting sick or injured with proper sleep, nutrition, and training. The next couple of chapters will be what I've gathered from years of trial and error, studying, passing exams, and what the current generation of professional athletes are doing. If you are concerned with anything in these chapters, please ask a medical professional's opinion prior to following what the content of this book recommends.

Before getting into physical training, players should spend the most amount of their time developing control of the ball. In previous chapters, we went over a brief overview of the idea of how to train as efficiently and effectively as possible. It is important that this principle is at the center of every session. If you look at other countries that do not have as many restrictions on kids going to school, they have tons of kids playing soccer all day, every day, no matter what. That is several hours a day spent playing, being on the ball, developing soccer awareness, and soccer IQ, that we miss out on in America. If our training is not efficient and effective, then America will forever have no hope in closing the gap on countries that already have a better structure for youth players or at least a structure that allows players to play all day.

To get the most out of training alone, it comes down to how many repetitions you are doing in a given amount of time. Let's call the number of repetitions volume. If we use the equation; Volume X Time = Intensity we can check how intense our sessions are in developing ourselves technically. If we do 10 reps in an hour, we will not be as good as the person doing 5,000 in the same hour. Through this amount of volume, the connection of the brain to the ball will develop more completely because you're placing enough stimulus on the brain and body to create an adaptation. You'll see very often, a group of players going to a field to train and they end up just taking turns shooting. A low number of repetitions in any amount of time is where a lot of players get left behind. Conversely, you can see a lot of players quickly eclipse others because of how much more they're doing in the same amount of time.

My favorite way of explaining the fundamentals of soccer training is by comparing it to a martial art such as boxing. It may seem ridiculous, but the two sports have a lot in common, and some of the similarities can be used to make your training better. In boxing, a fighter will prepare to put their health on the line during a match. This means the consequences of not preparing properly are profound, because they might sacrifice their health permanently if they are not prepared. If we look at how boxers train, they do a lot of volume in a short amount of time to prepare themselves to perform without having to consciously think about the movements and be able to fight using mostly second nature. This should be the same thing in soccer, training with a high amount of volume on the technical aspect, so that during a game, the skills are able to be performed as second nature, and the ability to create a command that turns into a successful play, is as fast as it can be if needed.

The same way a boxer will train using combinations on a heavy bag or hitting mitts with a trainer, soccer players should work on their combinations individually while keeping in mind how they translate into the game. For example, let's say a player plays left-back and is left-footed, they should work on the combination of taking a touch outwards, act like they are going to pass or shoot, and cut in, thousands of times because that is a combination of skills they are going to need to call upon in almost every game. The faster and sharper they can perform their combinations, the harder the job of stopping them becomes because the opponent can't practice defending against that combination as much as someone can practice using that combination. The same way a boxer might work on throwing a punch to the body and timing when the opponent covers their body firing off another punch to the head. If the boxer has a high number of quality reps under their belt, the opponent is going to spend a lot of time protecting their stomach while getting hit in the face. If we look at top-level soccer player's highlight reels, we see them doing a lot of the same moves repeatedly; sometimes to the point where the move is named after them. They set their moves up, and hit them on their opponents successfully and consistently.

This is from knowing what combinations work for yourself in your position and drilling them until the opponent can't really defend you, they can only hope you mess up.

A boxer will develop their own style to use to compete with their natural given attributes and will have the skills, concepts, and athleticism to back their style. As a player develops, it is important that they find their style of playing, and seek to constantly work on their strengths, weaknesses, and style. For example, let's say a player is smaller in size and is not that fast. Although it is important for them to work on their strength and speed, it is more important they are better technically, because that would allow them to play faster than other players can move or defend. You may be thinking about what happens when a stronger, faster player is also better technically? It does not matter. The player who is smaller and slower can keep up and have a better chance of success if they focus on what attributes strengthen their style of play and make them better. It is usually the players that have found the style of play that works best for their attributes, and reinforces their style with training, that find loads of success in soccer. If we look at Dani Alves, he has the most trophies out of any player ever on the professional scene. He is a very thin person, about average height, with decent speed. What makes him the most winningest player ever, is not that he is a better goalscorer than Messi or Ronaldo, or even close to being the best athlete, it is that he has found his style, and knows the way he wants to play better than opposing players can cope with. When he makes plays going up the right side of the field, he's done the same movement with and without the ball so many times that the opponent is almost helpless if they try to keep up. He has even dribbled past Ronaldo and megged him a couple of times.

In essence, players should train the skills, combinations, and concepts that work best with their style of play and positioning. If they keep this in mind during training and apply a high number of quality reps to their game, they will make progress faster and get closer to their full potential as a player rather than someone who practices random skills, and does not repeat the same movements that reinforce the style of play that works best with their attributes. This doesn't mean to never expand the skill set you choose to work on, this is to give guidance for what to work on. For example, someone who is very fast and plays left-wing, should work on receiving the ball into space and running past defenders full speed and either passing, cutting back, or shooting. Someone who is slower, but has a great ability to pass should work on positioning themselves to get enough space to find the pass.

Physical Training

When I started physically training I was about 13 years old and had no idea how to train for better performance. I would lift weights to get bigger, thinking that bigger meant stronger, not realizing that it wasn't functional to be bulky for soccer. If you look at players in the top leagues most players have a lanky, thin frame. This is a good body type for soccer because it makes it easier to run when you are carrying less weight, and more importantly, it is easier to change direction. Lifting weights and other methods of training do not benefit playing ability just because they are a form of exercise. The exercises for soccer have to be specific for how it translates into the game. This seems like common sense, but you'll see a lot of people do physical training incorrectly, and do more harm than good.

The first criterion for physical training is to make sure all elements of the body are healthy. If you have any injuries, or are suffering from fatigue, then you are going to end up doing more harm than good. I've tried the whole "overtraining thing" and it just leads to being tired and injured. When your body is healthy and you begin physical training, there is an initial phase called alarm reaction. Alarm reaction can be described as your body not being used to the breakdown in muscle tissue that the stimulus of training causes, and forces the body to protect itself by causing soreness. This soreness is similar to a bruise, with the idea that it is the body telling you something hurts and to not cause further trauma. The difference between the bruise and the alarm reaction soreness, is that most of the alarm reaction soreness is because of not being conditioned to cope with the demands of training, where a soreness from a bruise is from impact or trauma to muscle tissue. As a player gets more conditioned they are able to tolerate higher levels of stimulus in their training while taking on less soreness. At the beginning of physical training it might be tough to get through that initial alarm reaction phase, but once a player is past that, physical training becomes an enjoyable challenge.

A soccer player is required to produce force on several different planes of motion and the demands of the game call for several different athletic efforts such as; sprints, change of direction, jumping, etc. This makes the training for a player complex because they need time to work on the skills and in-game techniques while boosting their physical abilities. A great way a player can get the most out of a session, is to focus on different aspects for specific amounts of time during sessions. For example, if a player wants to improve their running endurance, they can run for 30 minutes at a moderate pace and afterward, work on their first touch. The trick to training efficiently and effectively is to make sure that what you are doing has enough focus so it can develop while it simultaneously does not cause overtraining or take too much time away from other skill sets that require training. The player that I am named after, Alfredo Di Stefano, has a couple of principles that he recommends for players to follow if they want to get better. One of the most important ones was making sure a player works with the ball every day. Even just doing ten minutes with the ball is worthwhile because it fires off the connection from the ball to the brain and maintains it instead of it getting diminished from not being used. A player is going to need to train physically especially as they get to the teenage level, but physical training should never replace technical training with the ball.

What type of training do soccer players need?

Before getting into the exact training methods we have to consider what a player does during a soccer game. They run, jump, cut, and perform skills from low to high intensities for different durations of time. Given that the player is eating the correct foods and getting adequate amounts of sleep in between training, a player would need to follow a general outline of training that inches them closer to being able to run, jump, cut, and perform skills for as intense and as long as possible without straining the mind and body.

There are 5 different categories of fitness a player should have understanding in:

1. Endurance
2. Core training
3. Strength training
4. Plyometrics/ Speed agility and Quickness
5. flexibility/ Recovery

Players must have some form of endurance training. You'll see a lot of players cringe at the idea of running because of the effort involved, but if you have a high level of endurance, you have better potential to get the ball in attacking positions and still have the energy to get the ball back on defense consistently during a match. At every level of soccer, it does not matter how good you are, you are not as good when you are out of breath or tired. This is a critical reason why you must train your endurance. There are many players who can play well for a limited amount of time, but when they start getting a little winded, there is no point in having them on the field because they can no longer contribute to the game.

To effectively and efficiently train your in-game endurance, I recommend two methods that have made a major impact on my endurance is a short amount of time. I went from coaches telling me I couldn't keep up, to being the guy who holds the record on the college fitness test for a top college-level team. The two methods are; long-distance low-intensity running and fartlek running. The reason someone would run a long distance at a low intensity is; it helps your body grow capillaries which makes your body's ability to circulate oxygen easier. If you run short distances as fast as you can, your body doesn't get a chance to develop these capillaries. The long-distance running is also beneficial because it won't promote as much physical strain. The long-distance run should be at a pace where you can maintain a conversation, and still be running. When you begin training long-distance running you might find it takes you a couple tries to find a pace that works for you. Stay in tune with how your body feels and keep track of your running by recording your distance and times. This data will be important to make sure you are making progress and to see what works for you.

The second method of endurance training, one that I wished I started training from a younger age, is fartlek running. Fartlek running is a Swedish term which means play with speed. The idea behind fartlek running is training at an intensity that would be difficult for you to maintain for an extended period, but only maintaining it for a short amount of time, followed by maintaining an intensity that is only slightly harder than a walk. During fartlek running, your heart rate will be brought up and down in a similar way to how soccer is played. The ball may not be near you for a couple of minutes, followed by a very intense burst of all-out sprinting and fighting for the ball. Fartlek running is the closest thing that I find to resemble the up and down intensity of playing in a real game.

Examples of Endurance Training

Jog at a talkable pace: 32 minutes: 4 miles: 8 minutes a mile
Fartlek running: 30 minutes: 2 minutes 80% of full speed: 2 minutes of 30% of full speed.

Core Training

The core of the body is very important to train because it stabilizes the spine and the rest of the body. Training your core can reduce injury risk and improve sprint speed, jumping, and strength. To train the core we have to first understand that its function is to stabilize the spine, control posture, and help with alignment of the body, as we perform movements associated with soccer in all planes of motion. Training the core begins with the alignment of the body, to make sure that our spine is in a good position, we have to be well versed in the drawing in maneuver.

Drawing in maneuver- This is also referred to as hollowing breath in and out. Gently and slowly draw in your lower abdomen below your navel, without moving your upper stomach and pelvis. As you begin to draw in your lower abdomen, keeping your shoulders back with a little tension will put you in a strong posture. It is important to understand that by using this technique, you'll better activate the core musculature and improve posture when doing core exercises.

Static Hold Core exercises

Plank	Side Plank	Quadruped	Floor Bridge

Dynamic Core Exercises

Leg Raises	Mason Twists	Bird Dog	Single-Leg RDL

Strength Training

Strength training for soccer stems from the understanding that the muscles in the body have to have high levels of endurance and be able to produce max-effort force in short amounts of time. Proper strength training improves speed, vertical height, and ability to change direction without injury. The most important aspect of strength training is the ability for it to increase the strength of the muscles and lessen the likelihood of injury, - nothing slows down progress more in soccer than having to completely take off from playing due to an injury. When beginning strength training for soccer, you should build a foundation of strength using your own bodyweight. Doing bodyweight exercises such as squats, push-ups, pull-ups, planks, and lunges can help build your foundation of strength. As players get older, and their growth plates are more established, they can begin training with weights and other resistance devices. If a player wishes to train with weights, the help of a trainer or fitness professional is highly recommended to ensure safety and good form.

Sets, Reps, And Rest

When starting, try to do 3 exercises for 12-20 reps for 3 sets with a minute of rest in between until you have a strong enough base to do heavier loads.

Bodyweight Squat	3 Sets of 15 Reps	1-minute rest
Push-ups	3 Sets of 10 Reps	1-minute rest
Pull-ups	3 Sets of 10 Reps	1-minute rest

Strength training and core training should take place on the same day. An entire full-body resistance training workout can look like this

Bodyweight Squat	3 Sets of 15 Reps	1-minute rest
Push-ups	3 Sets of 10 Reps	1-minute rest
Pull-ups	3 Sets of 10 Reps	1-minute rest

Plank	1-minute hold	
Leg Raises	3 Sets of 15 Reps	20 seconds rest between sets
Mason Twists	3 Sets of 15 Reps	20 seconds rest between sets

*Each time you exercise you should feel like it's challenging your strength. If the workout feels too easy, you're most likely not doing an intense enough workout for your current level of fitness. If the workout is too hard, and you're forcing yourself to overtrain, lighten the intensity by giving yourself more rest in between sets or fewer sets and reps.

Recommended beginner exercises for strength training

Bodyweight Squats	Push-Ups	Pull-Ups	Lunges	Bodyweight Rows	Nordic Curls

Key Concept to Keep In Mind when Strength Training

If an exercise is too hard, to where you can't keep good form while doing it, do not do it. The risk of injury goes up when an athlete tries to complete a rep of an exercise with bad form. To keep good form, always make sure that you are using the Drawing-in-maneuver and that your body is in good alignment before, during, and after a rep of an exercise. The instant you feel the exercise is causing a loss in alignment, take a rest or end the workout.

The lunge begins standing upright in a staggered stance. The knee that is behind the pelvis should go straight down, while the back stays completely straight and the abdominals are drawn in. The knee should drop to a 90-degree position, and then while pushing through the mid-foot, return to starting position.

Once a player has transitioned into lifting weights to increase performance, there can be confusion regarding what exercises work best, and what they should focus on to get the most out of training. In the book, "Underground Secrets to Running Faster" by Barry Ross, he brings up some very important points that relate to soccer players. He introduces the idea of mass-specific force, MSF. MSF is the idea that if two people can produce the same amount of force, but one weighs less, the person who weighs less, but produces the same amount of force, will move faster than a person who weighs more. This is a crucial concept for soccer players as they begin to transition into weight lifting. Soccer players need to maintain healthy body composition and try to improve their ability to produce force, while not gaining excess weight. To get faster, the trick is to improve the ability to produce force, while maintaining the same body weight. If you can produce more force, but gain weight, it negates your body's ability to move the mass that is your body. To train your body's ability to produce force, but not gain too much weight, you have to take longer rest in between sets and take on heavier loads.

Inside of muscles, there are different types of muscle fibers. When you are training to produce force, the main objective should be to train the fast-twitch muscle fibers responsible for producing force, and recruit as many motor units as possible. There are several different takes on how to train this aspect of fitness. Throughout all the books and courses I've read, and everything I've tried, the best method to train force production that I've discovered is the 5 sets of 5 repetitions with 85-90% of a one repetition max load, with 5 minutes of complete rest in between each set. The idea behind this is that resting for the entire 5 minutes gives your body a chance to reset the necessary energy pathways to stimulate force production. When you train with smaller amounts of rest in between sets you introduce the oxidative pathway, which means the training you are doing is more aerobic, with oxygen. This can lead to lactic acid build-up and create soreness. When you give yourself a chance to recover your anaerobic, (without oxygen), pathways you'll be able to focus on the muscle fiber recruitment that allows you to produce force and not get sore, or just mildly sore. This is very important because if a player trains too hard, and gets sore to the point where they have to take a couple of days off, they will miss out on time they could have spent training. The key to getting better faster is it train enough to stimulate growth and development, but never train so much that you face symptoms of overtraining such as; fatigue, extreme soreness, injury, or sickness. In short, it is better to underdo it than to overdo it.

The exercises that I have found to work best to increase power for soccer are the squat and deadlift. If you do not have the necessary equipment for a squat, the deadlift is the only exercise you need. The deadlift is the best exercise because you do not need a spotter if the weight is too heavy, you can just drop the weight. The deadlift works the entire posterior chain and the prominent muscles soccer players use when playing. If you were to do only one weight lifting exercise for soccer, the deadlift is the best. Before you attempt to deadlift or any other recommendation in this book it is important to consult with a medical professional to get the okay beforehand. If you are cleared to deadlift, it is best you start off with no weight and just focus on the technique. There are tons of videos online that can show you the proper technique to being able to deadlift, but a couple of key points that I recommend that you take into account are;

do not keep holding onto the weight if it is compromising your posture. If the weight begins to cause a collapse in your form during the exercise drop the weight ,and reduce the weight to an amount that allows you to maintain form and still stimulate the development of strength. For example, if a person's max deadlift is 100 lbs, they should try to work inside of the 85-90 pound weight range for their 5 sets of 5 reps with 5 minutes of rest in between. If they can not maintain decent form inside of the 85-90 pound weight range, they should drop the weight to 75-80 pounds and work from there. The very first rule of soccer training is, "Live to play another day." It is easy to let yourself over train, but it is important that you have the ability to train again tomorrow, or in some situations the same day. You can't get 100% better in one day. It is better to focus on getting a little better every day rather than train really hard, burn out, take time off, and try to recover back to where you were. By using the mindset of trying to train enough every day to get incrementally better, while still having the ability to train the next day, you'll be able to get better faster than most players because over the course of a year, you will have worked more than the players you are competing against. Starting off, train with the 5X5 method twice a week. You will know if you need more days of training, or to increase the amount of weight you are training with, by checking to see if you can beat your one repetition max. If you train consistently, but can't beat your one repetition max then you, most likely, need to do more.

Deadlift	5 sets of 85-90% of 1 Rep Max	5 repetitions	5 minutes of rest

Plyometric and Speed Agility Quickness Training

Plyometrics are training techniques used by athletes in all types of sports to increase strength and explosiveness. Plyometric training focuses on quick powerful movements for example jumping, bounding, or hopping, fall under plyometric training. There are 3 stages to plyometric exercises; the loading phase, the stabilization phase, and the exploding phase or the pushing off phase. It is important to keep safety in mind when training plyometrics because they are explosive movements and landing incorrectly or using bad form, can lead to injury. To make sure you lessen the chance of injury,make sure that you are warmed-up and hydrated first, and that you know the proper technique. Referring back to the strength training section, it is essential that you understand how to keep the body in alignment and land correctly.

Before starting to get into the more intense exercises of plyometrics, athletes should be competent in how to land. Landing after an explosive effort with bad alignment and lack of control increases the risk of injury.

To practice landing with a reduced risk of injury, an athlete can stretch as tall as they can and work on bringing their hips back keeping their abs drawn in and back straight. During this exercise, the athlete should focus on absorbing the force with the muscles by making sure they have good posture, and are landing with the midfoot while the hips are shooting back.

*Once the athlete has a good understanding of how to land, then they can progress into the vertical jump, broad jump, and other advanced exercises. It is important that an athlete develops their landing mechanics first. By being able to absorb more force, you can produce more force. Having the ability to absorb force reduces the rate of injury, because it reduces impact on joints, tendons, and ligaments.

Plyometric Progressions and Regressions Examples

Stretch and stick	Vertical Jump	Squat Jump
Side to Side hops	Bounds	Leaps
Single leg hops	Single-Leg Jumps	Single leg jump Landing on one leg
Vertical Jumps	Box Jump	Increased height on Box Jumps

Speed, Agility and Quickness Training

Speed is the ability to move the body in one direction as fast as possible. Agility is the ability to accelerate, decelerate, stabilize, and quickly change direction with proper posture. Quickness is the ability to react.

How much SAQ?

Depending on the training program and the session, SAQ training can be a couple of exercises, or the focal point of a session. Because SAQ involves maximum bouts of speed, it is best to give 20-30 seconds before each rep to make sure the player has enough rest and can perform close to max effort for each rep in order to force the body to adapt to the stimulus of speed, change of direction, and reaction.

3-4 exercises with rest 1 to 3 times longer than the duration of the exercise

SAQ drills for soccer

T-Drill	Box Drill	Triangle Drill	Mirroring	Pass Reaction

Flexibility Training

Flexibility training can be defined as the practice of making sure the muscles can function within their full range of motion without any pain or tightness of the muscles. The techniques available to make sure a muscle and joint can function in full range of motion are stretching and foam rolling. While warming up for a session, it's best to use dynamic stretching. After a session, static stretching can be used to cool down and keep the muscles from tightening up on the way home. The day after, exercise can leave you with soreness, using foam rolling can help relieve the soreness.

Dynamic stretching- using movements to bring a muscle to its full length. For example, leaving one leg on the floor with the knee locked and leg kept straight, while the other leg is kicked forward in a stiff leg, knee locked, position and then stepping and switching legs will bring the hamstring of the leg being kicked forward into a stretch.

Static stretch- Holding a position for a given amount of time that lengthens a muscle. For example, trying to touch the toes and holding it for 30 seconds.

Foam Rolling- In essence giving yourself a massage by placing your body weight on a foam roller and rolling over the tender area, or placing the tender area on the foam roller until you feel a release in tension.

Dynamic Stretches

Front kick	Side Kick	Back Kick	Quad 2-sec Hold	Butt Kicks	High Knees	Lunge and Twist

Static Stretches

Hamstring Hold	Quad Hold	Butterfly	Lunge

Foam Rolling techniques

Rolling on the; upper back, hamstrings, calves, adductors, quads, IT bands, glutes, Etc

Sleep

The first foundation of health, and arguably the basis of all health, is sleep. Sleep can be defined as two states: non-rapid eye movement (NREM)sleep which is subdivided into three stages (N1, N2, N3); and rapid eye movement (REM).

The first stage, and the one that takes the most time when we sleep is NREM sleep. NREM sleep is responsible for removing all the unnecessary information out of our brains. This is very important because it allows for the information that is important to stand out and be better absorbed.

The second stage of sleep is REM sleep. REM sleep is very important because it is during this part of sleep where the brain forms connections and helps retain important skills. All the training you do with the ball only works if you get quality sleep and let the brain do its job of getting rid of unnecessary information, and letting it build the connections that are necessary for skill development and cementing memories into our brain.

Understanding the two stages of sleep is important because it shows that we need complete sleep for the brain and body to do their job of recovering. If we reduce the amount of sleep we are having, we aren't giving the mind and body enough time to cycle through the two stages entirely, to remove unnecessary connections while cementing the ones we intend on creating. Reducing sleep on either end, whether it's going to bed late or waking up extra early, removes the ability for proper cycling of the two stages to repeat, and get the priceless use of a good night's rest.

The recommended amount of sleep is 7-8 hours for adults, and 9-10 for school-aged individuals and adolescents. The quantity of sleep doesn't matter as much as the quality.

Tips for better sleep

- Go to bed and wake up at the same time every day.
- Sleep in as dark and as quiet a room as possible.
- Get your recommended amount of sleep every night.
- Limit the consumption of caffeine and sugar before bed.
- Try not to exercise 2-3 hours before bedtime
- Never drink alcohol or do drugs.
- Try not to eat a big meal before bed.
- Don't take naps after 3 pm.
- Don't use electronics an hour before bed.
- Read before you go to bed to relax and fall asleep.

The Negative effects of lack of sleep

- Obesity in adults and children
- Diabetes and impaired glucose tolerance
- Cardiovascular disease and hypertension
- Anxiety symptoms
- Depressed mood
- increased age-specific mortality

Benefits of a good night's sleep

- Keeps your heart healthy
- Sleep May Help Prevent Cancer.
- Sleep Reduces Stress.
- Sleep Reduces Inflammation.
- Sleep Makes You More Alert.
- Sleep Improves Your Memory.
- Sleep May Help You Lose Weight.
- Napping Makes You "Smarter"
- Sleep May Reduce Your Risk of Depression.
- It helps reduce the risk of cardiovascular diseases.

Nutrition

If we eat foods that don't contain the nutrients we need, and we fill ourselves with salts, oils, and sugars, we are giving ourselves a severe disadvantage for getting better at soccer. As we train, we break down muscles, use large amounts of mental energy, and water. If we don't replenish our bodies from the rigors of soccer, we end up consistently breaking ourselves down without building back up. The process of habitually breaking the body down and not replenishing it with the appropriate nourishment, will result in injury, fatigue, and poor performance.

The process of fueling the body goes way further than just stuffing ourselves with things that taste good. The things we put into our bodies have a huge impact on our body's ability to function for performance and recovery. At the youth soccer level, you see a lot of players eating an unhealthy diet with the idea in mind "I'm young and I'm having fun eating junk food and staying up late." By having the mindset of being able to get away with poor lifestyle choices, you're weighing yourself down with bad habits that will significantly slow down your soccer success. If anyone was going to take anything from this book, I hope it would be this; the difference between being successful and unsuccessful is doing the right things consistently while staying focused on the goal.

What is nutrition and how can I use it to become a better soccer player and person? Nutrition is the process of obtaining the food necessary for health and growth. Not all foods are made equally, some foods can propel your body's ability to train hard and recover more completely than others. Our body is like a car, and when we eat we put fuel in the car to be able to drive. If we want our car to be able to drive fast and go further we need to put in the right gas. If we put sugar, oil, and salt into our gas tank we not only slow down our performance, but also create unnecessary inflammation and force our body to try and catch up to where our body should normally be functioning, instead of propelling it into better performances and quicker recovery.

Macronutrients occur in larger portions of the diet. There are three types of macronutrients necessary to fuel the body; proteins, fats, and carbohydrates. Each macronutrient plays a big role in how our bodies perform and recover. Protein is used to help repair and build muscles when they are broken down. Fats are used as a fuel source when doing long-duration aerobic activities such as soccer. Carbohydrates are the body's first line of energy from food when doing activities. Eating too much of any of these macronutrients forces the body to take the leftover energy from the food and store it as fat.

Rule number 1: stay hydrated, stay alive

During activities like soccer, especially on a hot, sunny day, there can be a big loss in water and electrolytes. Under relatively mild levels of dehydration, individuals engaging in rigorous physical activity will experience decrements in performance related to reduced endurance, increased fatigue, altered thermoregulatory capability, reduced motivation, and increased perceived effort. That's not to mention the harmful effects of severe dehydration. Staying hydrated is not only important for your ability to perform in sports, but essential for living a healthy lifestyle.

Are Gatorade and other sports drinks beneficial for recovery and hydration?

Gatorade and other sports drinks make claims to rehydrate the body using fluids containing electrolytes; this being said, when you drink Gatorade you're also consuming large quantities of chemicals and sugar. Eating too much processed sugar is unhealthy. The American Heart Association recommends limiting sugar intake to 100-150 calories or the equivalent to 6 to 9 teaspoons per day. This means that drinking 1 Gatorade can put someone over the recommended amount. Drink your recommended amount of water throughout the day and make sure to be hydrated before games and rehydrate afterward with water.

SOS is an easy acronym to remember when picking food. SOS refers to not consuming or being aware of eating sugar, oil, and salts. Eating too much of these can slow down recovery and reduce the ability to perform.

Chapter 9: What Gets Measured Gets Improved

In one of my favorite books, "The 15 invaluable laws of Growth" by John Maxwell mentions the idea of what gets measured gets improved. This idea means that if you have data to compare yourself over time, you can see what works in making you a better player. This is a concept I unknowingly would partake in with my father after every game, and when I would train. Everything from the number of errors I had made in a game, or the number of juggles I could make in a row, I would record. This made it easier to come to an understanding of what was an issue in my playing, and its current level.. For example, there was a time when I couldn't consistently control the ball out of the air. I would get one out of every six or seven controls correctly, and I couldn't figure out why. To improve upon this weakness in my game, I would go outside and punt the ball up 30 yards in the air and try to control it. I would keep doing the skill until I could get ten in a row with good technique. Through understanding the data and making adjustments until I could get 10 in a row without error, I was able to quickly tighten up that part of my game and even look forward to the opportunity to show off how well I could take a punt or chipped pass out of the air.

By understanding when there is an error and being able to hone in on why the error is occurring, you can make great leaps, but this comes from first having something to use to diagnose your game. If you have no data to go off, you will be caught in limbo when trying to understand if you made an improvement, instead of having clear facts to measure. For example, if someone is looking to improve their strength, but never takes note of what weights they are using when they are lifting, they will never know when they have made a new personal best. On the other hand, if you have up to date and consistent data you can learn more about yourself and the methods you are using to achieve goals. If you want a better first touch on the ball, see how many times you can fire the ball against a wall and control it successfully. If you want your first touch to be better under pressure, see how many successful first touches you can make after firing the ball against a wall inside a minute. This idea works across all of the aspects a player will encounter if they want to get better, such as; technique, strength, speed, cardio, in-game success/failures, etc.. I still look back on some of my notebooks on days I would train with my father, and reminisce about times where I made an improvement in a physical aspect, or on days I came close to a personal record and did not succeed, and was able to figure out why, and come back a week or two later and smash that particular record. The game of soccer is a journey, and you can better navigate that journey by documenting and learning from your own past failures or successes. This also goes for anything you are trying to achieve in life; create your own metrics of data related to your development, and keep trying to break your personal records. You will achieve much more than if you wander around and never know where you were, and how far you have come.

SKILLS TESTS

DATE	SKILLS	TIME	SCORE	Personal Records
	Juggling	5 Minutes		
	Boxes	30 Seconds		
	Pulls	30 seconds		
	Pump Fakes	30 seconds		
	Scissors	30 seconds		
	Cut Turn 5 Yard Distance	30 seconds		
	Top Ball Push/Pull	30 seconds		
	2 touch 5 Yards	1 minute		
	1 touch 5 Yards	1 minute		
	2 Touch 10 yards	1 minute		

"What gets measured, gets improved." -John C Maxwell

This is an example of something you can use to track and measure data. You can use this same template for other facets as well by just changing the way they are measured. For example, if you wanted to measure your cardio you could use the metrics of how long it took you to cover a certain distance, or the duration of your run.

Chapter 10: The Things No One Talks About

Relationships in Soccer for the Players

Your first coach will be your parents. Everything you know and who you are comes from the influence of those who raise you. If you have the ability to play, train, eat, and sleep, your parents have already given you so much. Always respect your parent's guidance and time. If your parents have something they want to ask you, or share with you, you should be focused on what they're saying because they have the best intentions to help you. If you don't agree with what your parents have to say do not shut down in frustration, throw up a block, and cause tension between you and your parents. An open mind is a growing mind. If you don't agree with something, figure out first if the reason you're not agreeing is understandable, and not because you got emotional when someone critiqued your game. When I was growing up there were many times that I would disagree with my father just to defend the performance I had because I didn't want to accept that I had played poorly. It takes a high level of accountability to understand the criticism and use it to your advantage.

Dealing with the Coach

- You show up early to practice and games.
- Focus and work hard every practice and game.
- If you have a question, address it in person by yourself when the coach has time.
- When addressing the coach, try to see their reasoning from their perspective.
- Make sure the coach truly has your best interest in mind.

Relationships in soccer For the parents

Soccer is a very social sport, and you are going to socialize in a number of ways with many people in and out of your nuclear family. The relationships you have with these people are a very important part of soccer. It is very important to understand when relationships are toxic or beneficial to navigate through the political world of soccer.

It starts in the Car. Conversations and the transference of emotion in the car, to and from the field, are the basis for what a soccer player and soccer parents' relationship becomes either productive or destructive. The exchanges between player and parent during car rides can either be a very tense or empowering time. After a training session or game, a parent can express a number of emotions which affect the joy that a player feels for the game. For example, if a player has an off day, and the parent expresses disappointment with their child, not only has the child realized a poor performance, but believes they disappointed their parents. This transference of emotion can take the joy out of soccer, and make a player want to quit. A child's value shouldn't rely on their performance. Soccer should be thought of as something the child wants to do and it is ultimately up to the child to get what they want out of the game. It's not the parents' job to create the spark of joy for soccer, but more importantly, to fan the embers of what the child enjoys, and provide a supportive environment where the player can thrive. There won't be a more dedicated time between player and parent for talking about what just happened and what they think about their current interest in the game than the car ride.

This time is invaluable and should be treated as such. To make the most out of these car rides, conversations should remain as logical as possible. For example, if a player had made an error in the game, a parent can ask what caused the error on that play, and allow the child to mull it over. After troubleshooting the problem, the parent can ask what might be a solution to that error. In a conversation like this, all the growth and understanding is coming completely from the child. An example of a negative car ride is where the parent tries to express something to the player that criticizes them and the player immediately puts a block up to not allow anything to penetrate. As the parent gets more frustrated about being unable to convey their perspective, the player also gets more frustrated with the same criticism, now seeing it as more of an attack than help.

To get the most out of the car rides the player has to want to review what happened in the game, and when that takes place, the understanding of what they did right and wrong has to come from them as well as the solution.

I've seen the parent trying to play through the player and fix every little thing the player does wrong. This method of ripping the individual down and solely focusing on the negative doesn't build anything, the same way if someone is trying to build a wall, brick by brick, and someone else takes the bricks off every time one is laid there will be no building of confidence, self-esteem, or joy for the game.

Take each error made as a lesson, and something to focus on when training. If you use the mistakes as things to adapt to, the player will grow. If the mistake is used to rip the player down, it'll take longer for them to recover and get better.

Coaches and teammates

A coach and team have a definite effect on a player. If a player is on a team and the coach exercises bias and doesn't see the player as an asset, the player can feel excluded. When a player is part of a team but feels excluded, or not as celebrated as the other players, they become distant from the result of the games and ultimately lose their passion. It's the thrill of all the hours spent developing something, being executed in a performance that leads to victory, that fuels a player's passion. If there is a void between the outcome of the game and the player, their passion will grow dull and ultimately they will seek that thrill in something else. When selecting a team, make sure the coach will celebrate all the players they bring on and encourage everyone to be attached to the outcome of the game. This will create a positive environment where the idea of being on a team can flourish. It's one thing to just be signed up to be around a group of players and a coach; it's a completely different thing to be part of a unit that works together to win as a team.

Things to Look for In a Coach

- When selecting a coach it's important to determine their reason for being there. For example, when I played academy soccer, a common occurrence was a coach having more teams than they could handle and giving a lackluster service. By having too many teams, and reducing the quality of the training and coaching, the person who chose to take on more than they could handle has revealed they are more interested in collecting amounts of money than the development of the players. If the coach is working under these conditions any extra effort to help the players will feel like an exhausting task because they're not there to build, but there to collect. Check if the coach is there to build or to take.

- Check the philosophy of the coach. It's natural for coaches to be emotionally invested in the team, but it can be a detriment to the development of the team if that emotion affects the coaches' long term decision making. What many coaches will say is, "We're here for the development of the players." Meanwhile, when the score of a game gets close, they will throw everything they said out the window, and step on some people's toes just for the result of one game. If a coach is truly invested in the players and cares about their development, the idea of success should revolve around how well the players are implementing the training into their performances. From there, the results of the games will come and can be reflected upon, not the other way around. Does the short term result of a single game oppose the coaches' stated philosophy?

- The dark side of soccer that people don't talk about enough is the back door deals that can happen when there's a lot at stake in an environment flooded with egos and status seekers. I've played at some of the highest levels of youth soccer, and I've seen these things happen at all of them. A parent will speak with a coach and offer something in exchange for unearned playing time. Whether it's gas cards, frequent flyer miles, money, etc. There are many coaches out there that will accept these things in exchange for unearned playing time. As much as I hate to say it, it's part of the game, but that doesn't mean you should get victimized by it. You can either address it or leave it, but understand no matter where you go, it'll be there. Just make sure that deal that's happening doesn't affect your well being in the sport. Depending on if the coach is on the take, or his political connections to the team are obvious, it is up to the player and the parent to decide if that environment is one where they can grow. I always thought working hard and being honest would save me from the dark side of soccer and even after I had done more in youth and collegiate soccer than most, there were still plenty of times I fell victim to the dark side of soccer.

PostScript: My biggest mistakes in soccer

It is impossible to have a perfect soccer career. You will inherently make mistakes. In this bonus chapter, I will express some of the biggest mistakes I made in soccer and things I wish I avoided. The first thing that I wish I did more of, was to build a connection with coaches or people who made decisions. There were many times where I was just as good, if not better than another player, but I was never able to move to certain teams or organizations because I had no connection to get me there. When I was trying out for professional teams going to tryouts and combines, what always became apparent was that I would go to these tryouts and not know anyone, meanwhile some people were already good friends with the decision-maker for the team. Not having an in, or having any serious connections makes it that much more difficult to make a team. Let's say that you are a little bit better than someone at a try-out, but they know the other player who you are competing with, and they have an arrangement where one player is the son of a guy who played for the team years ago. They are always going to pick the son of the guy who played for the team years ago because they have that connection. Even though you are a better player, probably worked harder, and have better accolades in soccer, you can't escape these types of things from happening. The only way to get ahead of political connections is to have your own connections with organizations or people.

A huge mistake that I made during my time in youth soccer was staying in toxic environments too long. When I was 14-16 years old I spent three years inside an academy that was not a good environment for me and it definitely stifled the progress

109

I could have made when I was developing as a player. When you are entering High School, it is important to make sure that you are playing soccer on a consistent basis in live game

situations. When I was on the academy team, I would be benched, or sometimes not even rostered to show up to games. If I had spent those weekends in actual live game situations, or even playing pick up soccer, I would have been better off, but in thinking that I was in a better environment, I stayed, even when it was obvious I should have left sooner. Evaluate your current situation with these criteria; you are playing frequently in live game situations, you're playing on a consistent basis with at least half the game worth of playing time, and your playing is not affected by another player's political situation or a coach's opinion. Soccer is a game of political opinion and connections, do not let this stop you. Just make sure that you have a decent living situation inside your team. During crucial years of development, I would have gotten better faster had I experienced those years playing in games, instead of just trying to survive a toxic environment.

The last thing I wish I had done more of was; evaluate soccer as a whole. When I was in youth soccer, I really could not get enough of it. I would practice every day with the ball, watch soccer, play video games that were soccer, read books about soccer, and even try to look like Ronaldinho, but what I failed to see was what soccer was at its core. Soccer at higher levels is a business first and a sport second. Even on top teams, players who are good, get pushed to the side for players who are more marketable and sell T-Shirts. If a major club wanted to expand its brand to parts of the world where soccer is popular, but that part of the world did not follow their club they will buy a player from that part of the world and play them to sell shirts and gain new fans for the club. This makes millions of dollars and it doesn't matter if a player is better than the guy they are bringing in to expand the clubs brand; they are simply looking for a big pile of recurring money, not who will give them the best result. Soccer is very similar to movies, you have actors who play roles in movies and because certain actors are in the movies, the movie makes more money, maybe a different actor was more suitable for the role. Had I known that the highest levels of soccer were more of a business than a form of competition, I may have spent that time trying to master something else like martial arts. This concept applies to many things in life, when you attach yourself to a group, it's comfortable to surrender to what the group thinks and does. Many players that go through soccer and see the route that everyone else is taking, usually end up taking the same route, without checking if it is in their best interest. Take a step back and see if the route you are on is ultimately going to benefit you, and is not just what everyone else thinks is a good idea.

My final thoughts about soccer are that I'm grateful for all the time I spent playing soccer. I learned many things about life, how to learn, and I wouldn't be the person I am now without soccer. What I realize now, is how much fun it can be to just go out and play without having to think about what a coach might think, or if the performance was good enough to earn more playing time in the next game. Soccer (without business), is the world's game, and no matter where you go, soccer is there.

Part II: A collection of Experiences from a Youth Soccer Journey

Bryan Muniz

Chapter 11:Introduction

When I started playing youth soccer for a travel team in the 70s, the cost of being on a travel team for one season was $15 and it included a T-shirt which served as an official home and away uniform. I was on the Woodbridge Warriors, and fiercely proud. I played high school soccer, NCAA Division 1 College soccer, and later, semi-pro.

Despite all the years, of drive time, playing time, and reflection on the whole soccer experience, I realized, at 40 years old, with 4 kids, that none of my previous time in soccer prepared me for being a parent of a youth player.

Still, I've been blessed. I can say now that some of my worst suffering as a parent came from soccer, which was not even that bad. I want to make clear that the ups and downs we went through in soccer, are nothing compared to the suffering of parents who have children that are sick, disabled, or have passed on. Also, what will become evident as you read on is that I am not an expert of any kind. I did go to college, (and graduated), but I'm a blue-collar guy. So, I'm just going to tell you what happened, and how it made me feel. I'm going to apologize in advance, because sometimes I get emotional and I cannot express myself as well as I would like. I keep remembering this guy Randy, at work, who paid for his own studio time to "cut a rap record" that (HE) thought was absolutely awesome. I'm well aware that what is important and meaningful to me, may not represent other people, and that what I might consider a quality explanation, may sometimes fall short.

Stefano is my 3rd kid, and first son. We've been on a 15 year, soccer journey that consumed plenty of time and resources. Many mistakes were made, but I also surprised myself and got some stuff right. My feeling as I write this, is that maybe I can help other people, and that by telling this story accurately, people who read it might be able to navigate youth soccer and get the most out of it, while avoiding some of the crappy stuff that comes with being a soccer parent or youth player. I'll be changing some names.

Why Soccer?

My father was born in the Cantabria region, in the north of Spain in 1927. The oldest of six boys, he started working full-time at age 12 in a factory that was on an island, which has now been turned into a golf course. To get to work, he would row a boat across a small stretch of ocean every day. People sitting in a café on the rocky shoreline would watch as he overcame the breaking waves. After work, he played soccer barefoot til dark with other kids in his town; they used a ball made by bundling rags tightly with rope. Even as an old man, he showed me a depression on the metatarsal leading to the big toe on his right foot and said, "this is from playing soccer (barefoot)."

One day as a teenager, he played in a game between his town and the next town over. Both communities would simply walk to the field and crowd the sidelines. That day, my father scored four goals for the win, and met my mother. During his mandatory military service, he was stationed in Africa, and played soccer on grassless fields that were so dry that some of the cracks on the surface were deep and wide enough to fit the arm of an adult. He said he loved scoring goals with his head, diving headers especially. Once though, he ran down an African opponent and prevented him from scoring by sliding on the ground to block the shot at the last instant, after chasing the man for half the length of the field. The field condition caused him to peel away a considerable amount of skin starting just above the ankle on his right side, and reaching the back of his right shoulder. Years later, he came across a commanding officer in their home city who recognized my father and shouted to him from a distance, "Adios Garrincha!" which my father interpreted as friendly sarcasm, contrasting my Dad's brutal enthusiasm with the smooth flowing style of the legendary Brazilian. I was always mesmerized by his stories.

Married, with two kids, my parents arrived in America in the 1950's. They settled in Newark, NJ where my father was spit on once, just for walking home from construction work, during the growing racial tension. Apparently, his white complexion led some black residents to treat him like he was the enemy, when in fact, he was just one more hard working immigrant like the other Spaniards, Portuguese, and Italians that lived in Newark. He had never been a racist or behaved in a racist manner, and in this new country, he was determined to overcome any discomfort to do the best he could for his family.

Fortunately for my father, my mother had been born in Pennsylvania.Though she was raised in Spain, my mother became the first person in our family born in America while my maternal grandparents lived in Pennsylvania, after leaving Spain to escape a revolutionary war. She was named America, and my parents were able to migrate to the US legally, as a result of my mom having been born in PA.

I was born in Newark in 1966 and as my father's construction business picked up momentum, we moved to Woodbridge, New Jersey in the early 70s. When we left, friends from Newark would look at my father in confusion, " you're going all the way down there? To live with the Irish? The Hungarians? The Germans?" My father would simply reply, "yep".

Sometime around second grade my father saw me throwing a pinky ball at a strike zone I made on our garage door. He asked me if I didn't like kicking a ball and practicing soccer. It hadn't occurred to me. Soon thereafter, I was kicking a ball up and down our driveway one day, when my father stuck his head out of the basement window and shouted into the driveway, "hey, you wanna see the best soccer player in the world?" Pele' had begun playing for the New York Cosmos. They televised the game and when I ran into the basement and saw Pele' running on that big green field, I was awestruck by the attention he was getting from the whole world, and my father. My ten year old brain could not imagine anything greater, and throughout highschool and even college, no other desire for my future was ever greater than being a pro player.

For me, that's why soccer.

Chapter 12: Ronaldinho

FC Barcelona Is widely regarded as the most beloved soccer team in the world. While the Franco regime wanted Real Madrid to be the flagship team for Spain internationally, (with the government financially backing the club); the Catalan region ran FC Barcelona through supporter memberships. The home stadium became a safe place for fans to speak out on political views that were considered controversial at the time. The club would not feature a paying sponsor on their uniforms for over the first 100 years of their history. Instead, the uniforms said UNICEF on them for years, a privilege paid for by the club. Club administrators insisted on entertaining the crowds by winning games while playing an aesthetically attractive style of soccer. Coaches who resorted to more rudimentary tactics were quickly fired and replaced.

By 2006, Barca supporters were being treated to the magical skills of a charismatic Brazilian named Ronaldinho. Nike commercials highlighted his skill, but also his contagious, friendly demeanor.

The Champions League final in 2006 was played between Arsenal of England and Barcelona. Barca triumphed 2-1. Jumping and screaming by my side, in front of our humongous tv acquired from the "going out of business sale" at The Wiz, was 9 year old Stefano. From that day forward, he began to imitate the gestures and moves of the Brazilian superstar, even copying his surfer-style greeting, with fist closed and thumb and pinky extended. It only dawned on me when I sat down to write this, that my son's reaction to Ronaldinho was almost an exact re-enactment of the first time I saw Pele' with my own father.

That year Stefano spent all of his time with a ball at his feet, at the bus stop, at school recess, after school in the yard, in snow, whenever. When I came home from work, we'd pass the ball back-and-forth in the front yard and I carefully watched his technique and got anxious when it wasn't precise. We worked mainly on trapping the ball out of the air, and dribbling. Many times, I figured the neighbors must think I'm crazy, but my obsessive nature about soccer made me keep pushing forward. I was sort of surprised that Stefano never complained, and he was so thick-skinned that he could handle any criticism or sarcasm that I would blast at him during the sessions. It was as if he didn't care how mean I was, but instead was laser focused on getting it right the next time. In a demented way, we were perfect for each other. He also quickly became a bit of a soccer encyclopedia. He knew which professional player was on what team and what trades were happening and which team was from which country, etc. I had a good laugh one day when he came home from school and told us that his teacher had been quizzing the class about which major cities belong to what country, and he was the only one who knew all the answers instantly. By knowing the teams that participate in each nation's league, connecting the cities with the country became second nature.

The most pleasant experience we had during those youth soccer years was rec league soccer. I found the coaches to be good hearted folks, and the other parents were humble and with a great attitude. They also had more reasonable expectations than any other team Stefano played on since. The first time we spoke with the coach, we told him that Stefano had never played soccer before, and he said, "that's OK, I've been doing this for years. He'll be fine." It was a nice feeling. Everybody was friendly. The season flew by and the games were fun to watch. Stefano celebrated his goals like Ronaldinho, and gave them equal importance. I was so proud of him. He played with an abundance of passion, and smiled all the time. He had shoulder length blonde hair, like his mom, and it looked really cool as he ran around on the field.

I should add that Manalapan was a step up for Ursula and I. When we first got married we lived in Woodbridge, which was a much older, much more blue-collar township than Manalapan. The boroughs in Woodbridge had a master plan that was far less attractive than the developments in Manalapan. Moving to Manalapan was a bit intimidating. Also, we observed at PTA conferences, that we were among the youngest parents around. It looked like everybody waited a lot longer than we did to have kids; probably in order to afford the sprawling colonials and bi-levels on huge lots in Manalapan. Either that, or it was grandparents attending the PTA meetings. New in town, with four kids, we felt immature. We had some money from family business, a bit of good luck on a couple of real estate deals, and my landscape business was holding its own. We had left the Fords section of Woodbridge looking for a bigger house and better schools for the kids, thinking it was the best thing.

Chapter 13: Travel soccer

Rec soccer had been a positive, comfortable experience, but I felt like it wasn't the real deal, so we found out about the tryouts for the travel team in Manalapan, and we showed up to the rec center, where A 20 something-year-old English guy sat at a table, registering the players. One of the questions that he asked each kid was, "what team did you play on before this?" I was rattled as I overheard some of the answers; kids were mentioning townships. In other words, they were coming from other traveling teams. When Stefano got to the table, the English guy asked him the same question and Stefano said, "the blue team". That was pretty funny, because that meant that he was coming from rec soccer, no travel soccer experience. Stef had no clue. Though I didn't think that it was possible for any other kid to have worked harder on his skills, I feared for my kid that maybe some of the other candidates were more experienced, or just bigger and faster. My only anxiety came from not knowing how my son would react if he were told that his journey to becoming like Ronaldinho, was going to end right there, that day, at the Manalapan rec center. The next day, we were informed that he had made the travel team. I consider this the point at which we really began to experience youth soccer.

There was a meeting at the rec center for all of the parents. These were NOT Woodbridge people. We all went around the table and introduced ourselves. The other parents were predominantly composed of two groups, one I will refer to as high-pitch whiners, the other, low-pitched aggressors, both from New York. I had no idea at that time, that Manalapan was also known as Staten Island South. When we first got the house, I was raking leaves outside when my neighbor yelled, "welcome to New Jersey!" I didn't get it, - I had never lived anywhere else except New Jersey, but, I found out later that most of my neighborhood was made up of transplanted New Yorkers.

Mike Mallet was the coach of the travel team. He also had a son on the team, and was also the president of the entire Manalapan soccer club. He stated that he'd never played soccer, but that he was a "student" of the game. He instituted a rule for the parents called "dollar a goal," so, every time the team scored, each parent had to pay a dollar. I didn't mind, whatever. The fees were already covered by the registration fees paid by the parents; maybe these extra funds would go toward something good. The transplanted, New York low-pitch aggressor Moms were not so subtle; "why do I gotta pay a dallah!?" I observed that Mallet didn't mess with those people. The team of 10-year-olds started playing in their league and doing well. Manalapan had a nice base of players to choose from, as well as ambitious, upwardly mobile parents providing the impetus for their kids to excel. Playing time for my son was strictly limited. When he played rec soccer, I was in a mindset where I wouldn't care how many minutes he played as long as he had fun. But, something changed in me when he made the traveling team. I saw other parents aggressively vying for position for their kid in the pecking order of the team. I was getting frustrated, Stef was in on one throw in, out on the next. It looked like playing time was based on who lived in town longer, or some other mystery process. My wife didn't like seeing Stef on the side for the majority of the game, wearing the orange pinnie for the substitutes. We noticed that when Stef scored a goal, it served as a reminder to Mallet to take him out immediately. My angst was compounded by knowing that Mallet did not know anything about the game. To me, it was pretty dishonest to get into coaching a sport that you didn't know anything about. I always sent my kids to the most experienced karate, Jiu Jitsu, and boxing coaches that I could find. To me, it would be reckless to get into coaching kids in something that I hadn't done myself. One day, after a game where Mallet put Stefano in, and he scored a goal within one minute, (and was taken out of the game immediately after scoring), I called Mallet at his job on Wall Street; I asked him if he thought that maybe Stefano should play at a lower level. (Although for me, if I had a kid who could score a goal within a minute of getting in, I would just leave him in for two or three more minutes). He said, "no, he's exactly where he belongs, I think that next year...next year (he repeated), the game will open up for him and he will have an easier time." Now I was getting mad. My kid had better skills than everyone else on the team, at the practices they juggled to start the sessions, the count wasn't even close; Stef would do 3 or 4 times more than everybody else without dropping the ball, he was scoring more often than his teammates, with a fraction of the playing time, and now a guy who had never played soccer for even one minute, was making indications about my kid that sounded like he was repeating something he'd heard someone else say. Soccer in Manalapan looked better from the outside. Close up, this parent-coach, parent-president, was more politician than anything else, kissing all the wives hello before the games. The British trainer who'd run the tryouts was there for the practice sessions, but Mallet would run the games, arms folded on the sideline like a soccer philosopher, seemingly analyzing the game, until the ball would eventually go off the field and come near him. When he kicked it, the truth about his soccer experience was exposed in one awkward motion. It looked like a Pelican trying to kick a soccer ball. It showed how far he really was from understanding what he had in front of him, which would not be so bad if it wasn't impacting the lives of these kids. I guess nobody knew any better, or they didn't care. Soccer, I'd discovered, had become prime lurking territory for people who don't know soccer, but can talk their way through, because most parents don't know what they are watching. In this space, Mallet could fashion the reality that suited him best, regardless of the truth. Which kid worked harder, which kid played better, didn't matter. Mallet used his position to serve himself. There was another guy in the area who made a fortune as a soccer trainer; not much of a soccer player, but indeed was a former male stripper who still maintained that long haired, gym, tan, laundry appearance. Unable to distinguish one thing from another, many local soccer moms felt that this fella was the best possible trainer for their children.

Anyway, some folks on the team had no reason to be disgruntled. The children of the low-pitch aggressors played the whole game. Their Dad's looked like bar-room-brawl specialists.The high-pitch whiners were aggressive about either calling, or even questioning the coach right there on the field after the game. Mallet would cater to those folks. I was no match for any of that stuff. I believed in an outdated style of thinking, where it would be better to just be better than the other guy, (and be able to prove it)- and everything else would take care of itself. Unfortunately, soccer is based largely on opinion; you can't submit your opponent, like in Jiu Jitsu, or cross the finish line first, like in running or swimming, thereby removing anyone's opinion from the equation. Soccer is a team sport, and the coach decides who plays, and who sits and watches other people play. So, if the coach is a parent- coach, with no soccer background, more often than not, he'll be serving himself first, his friends second, and soccer dead last.

I've seen a few parent coaches do a great job. My youngest son played for a team in Woodbridge that was parent – coached by a man named Sebastian Videla. Not only did the man have a passion for soccer, and know the game in every detail, but he would always wait with players who were waiting for their parents after practice, or actually drive them home himself, and make sure that they were in the house before he left. To this day, some of those players that he coached at age 11, still contact him from their various life paths. Military, college education, or work, Mr Videla had an exemplary and lasting impact on their lives through soccer. On the Manalapan travel team, I was really disappointed. I had hoped the coach would have some prior soccer experience, and be able to teach my kid something. In soccer, time is of the essence. The sooner a kid starts learning the details of the game and cultivating his touch on the ball, the better.

What we got with Mallet was someone who was good at pretending to know, all the while promoting his own agenda. That's what I couldn't handle. Maybe my expectations were unrealistic, but I actually expected experience, fairness, and honesty. I'd played in too many soccer games in my life to not notice what was happening. After a season with this deal, I knew it was time to move on, which is not as easy as it sounds. When I thought about keeping my kid in the same sport and just moving him to a different team, I had to look at myself and ask, "are you becoming that crazy soccer dad?, are you looking at your kid through the loving eyes of a dad? Maybe the coach is right?" Maybe, what if, etc. Fast forward 12 years, I'm very happy to have removed my son from that team. Most of the other kids never made it past highschool in soccer, one of the low-pitch-aggressor kids became a field goal kicker on a small college football team, and 2 more had College careers in soccer that were uneventful.

P.S. As it turns out, an employee of Mallet's soccer training business who was being shorted on pay, began to distribute newspaper articles describing how Mallet had been forbidden from ever working on Wall Street again, because he'd been found guilty of changing information on documents to defraud investors. Thus, he had his share of mess to deal with. I realize that this was not directly soccer related, but it speaks to character, and it tells me that my intuition was pretty good back then. My decision to remove my son from that team was a good one. Though the guy was a polished charlatan who fooled plenty of parents, he was also a criminal who'd never played soccer before, and not a good coach for my boy.

The takeaways from all this-

1.) an old buddy, taught me a great lesson. He said to me, "here's how you turn a negative into a positive. You can show your kid how things really work, how people can behave in a manner that is unfair and get away with it. You can show him that there are reasons why they are doing this kind of thing, and explain that better people do the right thing even when they would have motivation to do the wrong thing." I'd seen that Roberto Benigni movie, "life is beautiful". My first instinct was to try to insulate my son from evil in the world, like the dad did in the movie, but my buddy was right, it was better for the kid to start understanding how disappointing people could really be, right now.

2.) Strange, but true- the Moms were impactful. While my own wife was just happy after games, knowing that my son didn't get hurt, other moms got their noses way up into the management of the team. With well worked gossip and innuendo, they were able to band into cliques, to create their own reality. By cheering the efforts of the chosen ones that they had agreed upon, (even if they screwed up royally), and by ignoring or downplaying the efforts of those who were not their favorites, they were able to fog what was happening on the field, to the extent that an impartial observer would think that he had just walked into the twilight zone. Mistakes seemed to be rewarded, good soccer would be punished. None of them had ever played soccer before, I doubt they had ever bothered to watch a pro game, live or on TV, but they knew enough to use their mouths to manipulate the husbands on one sideline, and the coach on the other. To those folks who are offended by what I just said, you are the problem.

Chapter 14: Academy soccer

We left the travel team quietly, relieved that travel soccer was over. It had been an eye-opener though. I wondered if it were actually possible to elude the dynamic that we encountered on the Manalapan team. If every team was going to be like Manalapan, I don't think I could handle it. I feared that most teams would be this way; alpha families controlling the coach, with truly better players sitting the bench watching wealthier, or better connected kids play. From what I was hearing, there was always an alpha family running things in the background at any team. Funny, it always seemed to be the same damn people. A busy-body wife, with some type of administrative position, and a heavy set husband with an annoying stance of prosperity, standing with legs a bit too far apart and arms folded. One more thing, a track suit. The husband in the alpha family always wore a tracksuit. It didn't look like he'd ever been to a track- I dunno. What really pissed me off was when I would notice a family try to wedge themselves under the wing of the Alpha family to make things better for their kid. It reinforced that the Alpha family was in control when this would happen. I was surprised at how easily some people would surrender their dignity. I wanted to tell them, "you think they're your friends?, They're going to keep yelling at your kid anyway, believe me." In the grand scheme of it all, the alpha family always appeared to be doing some sort of cost/benefit analysis. If stepping on a few other families would make things better for their own kid, then it was a done deal. They would yell at other people's kids, try to talk up their own kids, and make them seem better than what they really were, then go to the coach in secret to try to damage the image of someone else's kid. About the only thing that I noticed that could make an alpha family slow down was "crazy". They were experts at manipulating words and paperwork, but they were very uncomfortable when you pulled out crazy and dropped it in front of them. Once, when one of these tracksuits was yelling at my son, I said to him "hey why don't you shut ....up?" After that, he didn't yell at my son again. Yet, it wasn't so easy for me to work up enough nervous anger to let words like that fly in front of a whole sideline of parents, and who wants to be doing that all the time anyway? So, I even considered a different path for my son, after all, the soccer thing came from me, and it didn't necessarily have to be the path for my son. This modern version of youth soccer looked like a hundred miles of bad road. It had evolved into a chess game amongst the parents that my wife and I were not good at, or even inclined to play. There were other things to do, other sports, music, whatever. However, it was about that time that we heard about tryouts for NALA. NALA was a soccer academy being run out of Holmdel by Tap Anos, who had been a professional player and had played in the World Cup. I had seen him play many times, both live and on TV. For me, he was soccer's version of Bruce Springsteen, a Jersey guy who was the best in his field, and had gone around the world to prove it. I wasn't sure if Stefano was ready to take such a big step up. I wasn't even sure what Academy soccer really was... it sounded like soccerzilla to me; would they practice everyday?, would each practice be 3 hours long?, would it cost more than tuition at a private school? Stefano was only 10, but he was aware of how hard he'd been working on his game, he was fearless, and wanting to try out. Also, I was in awe of Tap Anos, and was thrilled that at this moment in time, my own boy had a chance to play at an Academy run by this legendary player, so we went.

One of the nice things about leaving a team where you are not happy, turns out to be the renewal of hope that you get as you enter the next situation. It's a peaceful, cleansing feeling. While one coach may have preferred that you mindlessly kick the ball forward, you hope another may appreciate that you take an extra step to control the ball and deliver an accurate pass.

At the NALA tryout, 12 boys showed up. Needing 11 to field a team, they took them all. It would be the first time they had a U-10 team at this Academy, and the new coach was an unassuming, hefty Peruvian guy. The talk in soccer circles was that the Academy had been set to offer this age group the two years prior, but the coach was to be the aforementioned male stripper, who backed out on both of those occasions at the last moment, when he saw that he could not lure over some of the powerhouse players from other Academy teams that he had his eye on. Armando, the new guy, didn't seem to care about acquiring talent from anywhere. It sounds funny, but the stripper issue was a symptom of a bigger, more serious problem. The original intent of the USSF was for academies to develop players. They were actually called "development academies." When the moment of truth came, like the stripper, academies would just try to poach the biggest and best kids that they could get in any age group from other teams, to win games, appear to be superior instructors, and draw more business. Most rosters would be completely flipped in about 18 months, with the original team members being replaced by other players. In other words, the only thing the academies were developing were their own profits. Who would've guessed it? We took the world's game, which can be played by anyone, at any economic level, anywhere in the world, and found a way to make it into a profitable business, where the wealthy would have an easier time participating. Kids who weren't growing as quickly as others were told that, "The Academy is moving in a different direction and that they might want to find a different team where they could get more playing time." It was a lie to bring on bigger players, which was always the default tactic in the US, and much easier than actually developing players. There's no telling how many great players have been overlooked because nobody wanted to take the time to cultivate a player who can't help them win some meaningless trophy, this weekend. The academy structure also lent itself to making it possible for people to buy a spot on an Academy team that they didn't deserve. Some people of means would leverage favorable situations for their own kids by privately bankrolling several of the other players, who couldn't afford to cover the fees, and were theoretically at the Academy on "scholarship." Once, when the kids turned 15 and Tap Anos became their actual coach, a parent who I trusted had confronted Tap Anos on the phone regarding the outcomes of practice scrimmages where the "B" team would beat the "A" team for several weeks in a row, and yet, there would be no change in the lineup for the games; on that phone call, Tap Anos admitted that there were certain players who did not belong on the Academy team. Why were they there then? I can't say. The fact is though, that there were some players coming from a very high socio-economic level, children of plastic surgeons, for example, who were starters on the Academy team, and yet were not able to get many minutes of playing time on their own High school teams; which should have been a much easier task, being that high school soccer was at a much lower level. One plastic surgeon actually became the official Doctor for the Academy. Huh? Like having an auto body shop be your official mechanic, I dunno. Anyway, his kid was a starter at the Academy, and a bench player at high school.

The cost of being on an Academy team was approximately three times more than being on a township travel team. I hoped the higher cost would translate into better results. In 2008, the cost was about $2500, which seemed like quite a bit, but my mind-set was full steam ahead. I would've done whatever it took to make it work.

The practices were immediately more intense through Armando, the Peruvian coach. He took a liking to my son's ferocious work ethic and made him the team captain. Imagine that! From five-minute-a-game bench player on a travel team, to captain of an Academy team. The world is a funny place to begin with, and the world of soccer is funny too, and absolutely incomprehensible. The first tournament was somewhere in Pennsylvania. NALA played against much tougher teams than any traveling team my son had played against. We won the tournament. My son was the team captain, played the majority of the minutes, and finally felt a vested interest in the results and the context of the games. By the end of the weekend, I had told my wife (more than once), that I would've paid the $2500 just for that one weekend. As a bonus, we had left behind Mallet, his politics, and his lack of soccer knowledge. Two other players from Manalapan had also left the travel team, joined NALA, and they were actually old friends of Mallet's. They told me one day at practice that Mallet had expressed to them, that he was truly upset that they had left the Manalapan travel team, because he had treated them like family. Well, I guess Mallet knew he had not treated my son and I like family, because he never said stuff like that to me. Instead, he told his old friends that he couldn't believe that the Academy had taken Stefano. The narcissist actually thought that his opinion still mattered.

Soon, it was time for NALA to play against Manalapan at Manalapan's home field. Cunningly, Mallet chose the smallest field in the complex to play on, hoping that NALA would have less room to work their passing game, giving Manalapan some sort of advantage. It was awkward seeing people from the Manalapan team that we'd shared the sidelines with not long before. My mind was stuck somewhere between "ok, we're all adults here, no reason to behave in a petty manner" and "I hope we unceremoniously beat the hell out of you." In the end, NALA won the game; for me though, there was a bigger issue. My son scored the game winning goal. In youth soccer, nothing says, "you got it all wrong", louder than your last bench player from a few weeks ago, coming back to your home field as Captain of a better team, and scoring the game-winning goal against you. One of the other Manalapan refugee dads came to me after that game and said, "Now that must feel good huh?" On that day, I only smiled in response, but whenever I reflect back on that moment, I get a dopamine hit you wouldn't believe. Not sorry.

That season the Academy team bristled with excitement. The parents looked at it like their kids were automatically at a higher level just by being on an Academy team. For a time, they had good reason to feel that way. Whenever we went to a tournament, the boys would usually win. They even beat more established Academy teams from North Jersey. Township traveling teams were routinely slaughtered. This success seemed limitless. Parents at the Academy seemed to feel special and privileged. Including me.

To his credit, the humble coach Armando achieved these results by just working with the 12 boys who showed up at the Academy try-out that first day. He had not tried to lure players from other academies over to NALA, or poach good players away from their travel teams, which was truly noteworthy, a testament to Armando's understanding of soccer. Poaching of course, was illegal as per NJ Youth Soccer, but everybody was doing it. Ironically, for our team, there were certain advantages that came with having a small roster. The one boy who was the substitute most of the time, didn't seem to mind. He knew that he was not quite ready to play at that level, and occasionally told the coach that he didn't particularly need to go in to the games. Therefore, there were no arguments regarding playing time. Actually, I think that by each kid having a specific role on the team (that he didn't have to share with anyone else), they may have all sort of "risen to the occasion", having a clear-cut job to do, and defend, with pride. I could actually see it when they played. We got damn lucky. If we had stayed with Mallet, we would've still been invisible and miserable.

The next three years at NALA saw distinct changes in the players themselves, parents, and the administration of the Academy.

From age 11 on, the varied growth rates of the boys become pretty extreme, some will be adult size, others will still look like children. When this starts happening, even the most knowledgeable people in soccer can be fooled. A kid who's got the jump on puberty and growth may cover more ground, and will always appear more adept at collecting the ball and moving around the field. When colliding with smaller players, the larger guy will become an invaluable asset in the eyes of the parents on the sidelines. The balancing occurs as the kids mature, the differences in size become lesser, and less advantageous. Then, skill, speed of thought, and coordination start taking over. You would need a crystal ball to determine if the player with the size advantage today, will still be a dominant player tomorrow. Again, most people won't be looking past the weekend. I have friends who have reached high levels of international soccer who say that when they were younger, they were certainly not the best player on their youth teams. Countless top-level players throughout the world tell stories of being let go from their teams or being turned down by prospective teams, only to have those same teams pay exorbitant amounts of money to retrieve them later, when their abilities became more evident, and their stature less important. So it shouldn't be a shocker that playing time starts going haywire during adolescence for these youngsters. In addition to the disparity in growth rates, growing pains will commonly create discomfort just below the knees and occasionally inhibit training.

It's crucial to see past all this. Johan Cruyff, the iconic Dutch player and Barcelona coach, would say, "first the player, then the athlete." Meaning, first we should work on skill, soccer IQ, and gamesmanship, and the athletic elements can be obtained later. Unfortunately, parents as well as coaches want to win now, right now, this weekend, this season; so everybody goes for the short cut, and some skilled players get brushed aside. Developing smart players can't be a consideration when there are tournaments to win, and the kids will be with the same coach for only a few months. So, putting bigger players on the field works, until it doesn't. The kid with the mustache at 13 may look like he has an advantage over the 12-year-old who still looks like a baby, but that evaporates quickly at around 16, and neither player should be punished. Every step should be taken so that the more physically mature player keeps working hard to cultivate his touch on the ball, and speed of thought on the field, so that he's not unarmed when the other guys catch up on the growth curve. The less physically mature player with good ball control and coordination, should be encouraged to continue to play during this phase, expand his vision of the field and play recognition. My son Stefano was born in December, conceding almost a year of growing time to some teammates. We weren't thinking about sports when we were conceiving the kids. There are families throughout the state however, that have all male children, all born in January. We didn't even know you could do that. My wife and I are average sized people though we have giants as well as tiny people on both sides, so my son grew up behind the growth curve and did suffer the effects of being smaller than the rest. I know some parents that decided to pursue growth hormone treatment, and others who kept their kids back in school up to 2 grades to gain a size/strength advantage for high school and college. Some folks coming over from Latin American countries had a distinct advantage of coming from infrastructures where birth certificates were, well, sketchy. So, those kids were sometimes actually older, not just growing faster. Parents of other kids on the team were quick to point out that Stef was falling behind in growth, disparaging Stefano to the coach behind our backs. How things had changed in a year or two. By 17 though, Stef was a hulking 175 lbs of muscle at 5'9" and ripped. The boys that towered over him a few years before may still have been taller, but didn't stand a prayer of dispossessing him of the ball because of the difference in raw strength and skill. Again, there would be no way for anyone to know that that was going to happen, and the five years from 12 to 17 had some ugly times.

ODP

In 2008, The only place to go for higher recognition and competition than Academy Soccer, looked to be the Olympic Development Program. You can find out about the history and design of the program ot : usyouthsoccer.org. Coach Armando had encouraged Stef to try out. I was hesitant, once again wanting to shelter Stef from possibly getting turned down. My anxiety grew. It felt like "Oh no, another tryout..." It seemed like there was always a tryout. Maybe it was just my perception. Eventually, when the emotional consequences of not trying out became stronger than the emotional consequences of going for it, we went forward.

Tryouts were on a Saturday and a Sunday and players signed in and were given a bib number similar to the numbers given out at a 5K run. Evaluators with clip boards would stand on the field while the boys played, and took notes. One of the men who ran the program, Rick Meana, gave an introductory chat for the parents. He mentioned some of the famous players who had gone through the program Claudio Reina, Tap Anos, and, (even though she'd been cut the first four times), Carly Lloyd. He said , "Do we make mistakes?, yes, sometimes we do." Right there, my stomach felt weird. Butterflies, but also like I had swallowed a cannonball. He went on to say that, "it's not the easiest thing in the world to tell a youngster that he's not yet ready for a certain level of competition." Ok. Reasonable. Understandable. Also, parents were not to talk to their kids or the evaluators during the tryout. I liked that. Mr Meana also stated that, "we're not necessarily looking for who can get from here to there the fastest...we're looking for soccer players." I liked that too.

They broke the group down into small sided games. I told Stef something beforehand that I had never heard from anyone else before, or since then, and I do recommend for try-outs. I told him, " Try to keep the play in front of you. Try to always have a picture of how the play is evolving on the field in front of you, don't be looking over your shoulder to receive vertical long passes." At tryouts, a lot of players and parents think that the evaluators will only be noticing kids who score goals. I know this because other parents have told me so. They encourage their kids to think along those lines. It's not a good idea; they hang around upfield chasing the ball down on long passes that are basically a 50-50 raffle between themselves and the opposing defender. By age 12, most decent defenders are able to alleviate attacking pressure by passing the ball amongst each other, making an overzealous attacker look like a chicken running around with its head cut off. They spend the tryout doing more chasing than playing. By maintaining a central position on the field with the ball in front of him, Stef was able to make a well informed, successful decision when the ball arrived at his feet. This allowed him to showcase his touch on the ball. On one play, he even juggled it over some kid that had come in way too hot and over-committed himself. I took a quick look at the evaluator and saw him writing something on his clipboard. Yeah baby. For those two days, Stef stuck to the strategy, and was able to show his skills and high soccer IQ. His bib number appeared on the web sight the following week. He made ODP. Eureka!, someone with no agenda that I didn't know, had seen what I was seeing. My convictions about it being better to just be better, had been validated. Also satisfying was the fact that some of Mallet's old pals, the ones who tried to trash my kid at the Academy, didn't get chosen. Again, had we stayed with Mallet....

I knew some people who had a teenager who had made ODP also, and they told me that their kid had received six offers in the mail from college recruiters within a few days of making the ODP roster. I was pretty happy to hear that, even though my son was still too young to start looking at schools.

The practices at ODP were very structured and looked very professional. Most of the players behaved with reverence for the situation and respected the coaches. Those who did not, were quickly asked to leave. The practices were held at TCNJ campus which was approximately 45 minutes from our house. I didn't care, I would've driven 10 hours. It was that meaningful to me at the time.

Looking back, it might have been a smart economic move to play on a regular, quality travel team, then make ODP, and participate in that program to take advantage of the superior training, recognition, and overall experience. One would have to individually gauge how much better the chances of making ODP would be if you were practicing and playing at an Academy between ODP tryouts.

The state ODP teams in the area would train and play each other in a sort of mini-tournament, at Kutztown University. You would drop off your 12 year old on the beautiful Kutztown campus in PA, and for a week, he would train with great competition. Parent chaperones were invited to volunteer. I didn't. The value in this, in my opinion, was in the regimented process. A kid would set an alarm, wake up on his own, feel the exhaustion on his own, and figure out how to perform to the best of his ability the next morning, on his own. What a fantastic experience. Stefano's game improved more during his time at OPD than any other time in his life. I attended his little brother's karate tournament during that week, in Fords NJ, and some acquaintances asked me where Stefano was. I said " He's in Pennsylvania with OPD." "What's ODP ?," they asked. I answered, "The Olympic Development Program." They said, "Bryan, you got some talented kids. " That really felt great. By the end of the week, Stefano had been chosen for the Region 1 team. That meant that after evaluating all of the players in his age group in the Northeastern United States, Stef had been selected to be on the team to best represent one of the 4 ODP Regions of the country. I'm not exactly positive on the borders but roughly, it broke down like this : the Northeast was Region 1, the South was Region 2, the Central US was Region 3, and California was its own region, Region 4.

The four regional teams would play each other in a tournament during Thanksgiving weekend in Florida, at a place called the Proving Ground. This was a gorgeous soccer complex and an extension of Disney, with tons of perfectly groomed fields in different sizes, lights, pathways, stores, and more. Jersey had already started getting chilly, so getting off the plane in toasty Florida to watch my son play soccer, (and then renting a Ford Mustang to drive around), made me feel like I was hallucinating. The team stayed at the Radisson. Parents were allowed to attend, but only in hotels separate from the kids. Contact with the players was discouraged. My wife stayed in NJ to have Thanksgiving with the rest of the kids and their Grandparents.

The program was sponsored by Adidas, the kids all got free Adidas Predator soccer cleats and gear. Stefano pointed out the he was sort of sponsored by the same company who sponsored Xavi, the genius Barcelona playmaker. Yeah, sort of...

This was all pretty awesome, and it was even more dignifying personally because Stef was born in December and so was in a size/strength disadvantage because ODP worked on a calendar year starting on January 1st and ending December 31st.

The great Colombian soccer coach, Francisco Maturana, said, " soccer is a battle between who you really are, and who you think you are". That statement is pretty succinct, but it captures the entire mystery of soccer in a few short words. Many times, a guy can think he's accomplishing something, or being effective in some way, while actually being a detriment to his team. Reconciling both sides of the equation, who you really are versus who you think you are, becomes a different path and different destination for each player. When you're lucky, maybe you can settle in to a certain role as a youth player and progress peacefully. Others may battle through all the way. I would add that in youth soccer, if you don't figure out who you really are, there'll be plenty of people lined up willing to tell you who you are and put you in a place that fits their agenda, not yours. That's the value of taking chances and doing tryouts; escaping the grasp of those folks who will try to tell you who you are. In Stef's case, we had carefully pushed forward from rec to travel, to Academy, to ODP. It was stressful, but worth it.

That Thanksgiving weekend of 2009, ended with Region 1 beating the other 3 ODP regions and leaving the tournament overall winners. The quality of play, with all these screened players and great training, was a pleasure to watch. Stefano, who was already a skinny kid, actually lost weight during the weekend. The pants he wore on the plane were looser on the way home. I laughed and asked him what they gave them to eat, and he said, "mostly rice and salad." I doubt that, but I guess that's what HE ate.

The whole OPD experience is one big, sunny, happy memory. I feel the professionalism of the program and the separation of the parents from the coaches, as well as my son's abilities, made for a great experience for Stefano at ODP.

When the boys turned 13, the next coach at the Academy was a small British guy. He'd been here in the US since the 80s, but had maintained that wonderful accent. He was a devoted supporter of a British style of soccer that had been different from the rest of the world for the last 50 years. While most teams around the world began to adopt a more controlled version of soccer, with shorter passing and more precise team play, England entertained the world with their distinct style of high tempo running, and smashing of the ball forward. In fact, in a study to determine which national squad was the most watched throughout the world, it was not surprising that Brazil was the team that most people would tune in to watch. That nice, controlled style of passing and smooth flowing team play, was the envy of the rest of the world. Second on the list surprisingly, was England! Though they hadn't won a major competition since 1966, the use of large, athletic players who appeared to want to win only through brute force and superior morale, was a great draw for soccer viewers.

Many quality players had left the Academy during the time that the little British guy had been their coach. Most had jumped over to Red Bulls, apparently to come back and obliterate the little British guy's teams at NALA. He appeared oblivious to the 11-1 losing score against his former players. He enforced a "no watching" rule for the parents at practice. Can you imagine? Charging somebody three grand to coach your kid and then saying, "you can't watch what I'm doing with your kid." I found out from Tap Anos later, that so many parents had complained about the little British guy in previous years, that he'd decided to ban parents from the practices. Imagine signing your kid up for Karate, or boxing, and the instructor saying, "ok you have to leave now?", I should have taken that as a sign that something was seriously wrong, but I hoped that maybe the coach was just trying to reduce the influence of the parents regarding playing time. If we could hold on for one more year or two, then Stef would reach the age when Tap would be the coach, and that would be an epic moment. Myself and a few other parents would just walk or jog during the little British guy's practices, abiding by the "no watching rule". That part wasn't so bad, we'd commiserate about the coach, and talk about the games. I still talk to some of those guys. Soccerwise though, it was the worst time for us; Stefano wasn't that big and strong and it looked like the little British guy only wanted to field the biggest players. It was pretty easy for me to build up contempt for the guy, but, to be fair, he wasn't the only proprietor of this type of crap. Most youth national team players are born in the first quarter of the year, which translates to a size and strength advantage growing up, which leads to being selected for better teams or programs with better training, which leads to more advanced placement down the line. It looked like an over-simplified approach. Many times the little British guy told the boys to "just boot the ball forward," that it "wasn't a good day for intricate football, " which I believe was his term (intricate), for using intelligence on the field. I'll give the little British guy one thing, he held on strong to his beliefs; Once, we drove to a game in Connecticut. It was about four hours each way. Stefano played approximately the last 45 seconds of that game. I used to think he would've been better off staying home that day. He certainly would have run more than 45 seconds and done some good training with the ball, but now I cherish that experience, because of what came later, and because of how it shaped my son's character. Stef got to witness what I described earlier by living it; he was small, but he kept working, and he overcame the experts. When everybody leveled out on growth, he shot right past the big guys because he'd cultivated his skills first, leading unexpectedly, to a more successful college career than the players that had been favored at the Academy due to their temporary size advantage.

The little British guy was also a big fan of the offsides trap, which would've been ok, except that he used it as his only form of defense. Opposing teams would attack us, and our defense would soldier forward as per the coach, trying to trap the opponents in an offsides position. The problem was that it would only work once, then the opposing teams would recognize the situation and simply hold onto the ball and dribble right through for a free breakaway with our goalkeeper. Games would normally end up 3–0 in favor of the opponent within the first 20 minutes. Some of the other parents called it criminal. I would say that it was just foolish, and demoralizing. We lost almost every game. The little British guy made the opposing teams look better than they really were, because the boys followed his instructions, and played backwards. Stefano struggled through those seasons, with minimal playing time, in the hopes of eventually being coached by Tap Anos. In about 3 years, roughly 17 entire teams, boys and girls, had jumped ship to different Academies to avoid being coached by the little British guy. If I ever had such poor results in any endeavor, I would change occupations.

The takeaway from this:

Outlasting hopeless times will make you stronger, and the friends that you make in these tough situations, tend to end up being better friends than the ones you make when everything is going well. Stefano maintains a relationship with a teammate named Malcolm who basically found himself in similar circumstances. Malcolm was a very skilled player at the Academy who was losing playing time because the little British guy was apparently favoring players who he thought might help him more in a proper bar fight on the mean streets of Liverpool. To this day Malcolm, Stefano, and I still marvel at how perfectly backwards the little British guy got it- the guys who he favored, went nowhere in college soccer. Most didn't even make it to day one. Meanwhile, Malcolm and Stef, who had to spend their weekends traveling a few hours to sit the bench and watch the taller players play, had good college soccer careers, then, semi - pro and pro experience. We've agreed to put the roster on paper denoting the college soccer careers of each of the little British guy's favorites and deliver it to him, "here are your results: you got it completely backwards." Turns out, the little British guy doesn't work there anymore, and we're going to have to ask around to find him. This was something that I never thought could have happened with Academy Soccer. I thought that the reason to pay the big money was for a more accurate evaluation of the abilities of the players. As it turns out, you could pay three times the amount of the cost of travel soccer and still be misjudged due to the biases of the closed minded. In the case of this little British guy, you could cultivate some great soccer skills, enough in fact, to embarrass the six footers at practice every week, but if the guy is still thinking England during the late 60s, you're done. Stef and Malcolm still enjoy a fine friendship and professional working relationship.

Tap Anos once said, "I don't know any coaches who don't want to put good players on the field." Now there is a statement which sounds logical enough to lock out anyone else's opinion. The problem here is that the train of thought stopped a little short of its final destination. What if the coach's perception of what constitutes a good player is completely whack? What if the choices this coach makes regarding player selection and tactics are so off, that it renders his squad unable to compete with their peers? Then, you could reason that there are coaches who, like Mallet, have their own agenda, or, like the little British guy, have a distorted view of reality, and by extension, do not want to put good players on the field. I've seen em do it.

This brings me to a piece of advice that I am going to offer here that I wish someone had given me, way back then. While you're having your child play soccer, or any other team sport, consider getting them into an individual sport. During the reign of the little British guy at the Academy, Stefano asked to join his brother at Brazilian Jiu Jitsu classes. I could never overstate the value of this decision during this particular moment. It was exactly what we needed. At the academy, we were hanging on to an ideal that was fading away a bit more every week; that Stefano had earned a place at the highest level of youth soccer in America and that this was the place that would help my son to get to the next level. What we failed to realize was that Academy ball was just a business plan, that you're on your own, that nobody is coming to help you, and that this expensive, time consuming process could do more harm than good.

At jiu jitsu, Stef could use his ability to learn, and his discipline for training to excel past his peers. Nobody's opinion made any difference. This was in tremendous contrast to being in the academy, where opinions could easily asphyxiate you and leave your dignity blowing away like garbage in the wind, even if they were wrong. One day when he'd gotten some training under his belt, Stef told me that he wanted to compete in a Brazilian jiu-jitsu tournament. The tournament would be held in Montclair, New Jersey and it just so happened to be taking place on the same day as one of the Academy games. While we contemplated the logistics of missing a game, Stef said to me, "If I go to the Jiu Jitsu tournament, I'm definitely starting that day." Meaning that, unlike at soccer, there would be no coach there to stop him from engaging wholeheartedly in the competition for however long it lasted, and that no one besides himself could control how far he went. It was a Godsend. He won the tournament in impressive fashion, but the best thing was that he had rediscovered a way to succeed through his own efforts, in a way that made some sort of sense. He wasn't attempting to earn the privilege of being a piece of a machine assembled by someone else, instead, in jiu jitsu, he was the machine, built by, and for, himself. Even if he had not won the tournament, there was still something there. He learned a way of fighting and got to keep the confidence that comes with it. What a deal.

Whether you have boys or girls, I highly recommend Brazilian jiu jitsu, Karate, or boxing training, to be interwoven with soccer as a way of liberating your child from the politics and constraints of being part of a team, at the same time becoming an even more valuable part of that same team by becoming a better version of themselves. As a bonus, the kids may acquire some valuable skills in self-defense that may come in handy for a much longer period of time than soccer. Nowadays, with athletes making their lives more public, I've noticed that many top soccer players have pursued martial arts concurrently with their careers. I personally would've never guessed how complementary martial arts training could be for soccer, or how participating in an individual sport could save your spirit from the dark aspects of being on a team. I saw it reinvigorate my son, offering him a place to find joy when the academy and soccer itself were suddenly looking like a dead end.

Prior to the start of the following season, the USSF had decided to make regional leagues out of teams with Academy designations. NALA would be a member of the Northeast academy league. For ages 13 and 14, it would be considered pre-Academy and then full academy soccer for ages 15 and up. At NALA, Tap Anos would be the coach of the full academy team once players reached the age of 15. There was a meeting at NALA, supposedly to review the new format with the parents. Tap Anos was there to present his thoughts on the subject and answer questions. He also mentioned that these changes would now render ODP obsolete. He said that playing in high school might be a choice for those who enjoy the social aspects, but that it would not do as much as the Academy when it came to getting somewhere in soccer. He concluded by saying that NALA was basically the best option, because it was the only Academy in that particular area of New Jersey.

Stefano endured the 2 seasons with the little British guy. Nobody ever looked better in the rear view mirror. Now, now was the real deal. Stef was finally old enough to play for Tap and no mistakes would be made. My son would finally get a fair deal and his stature wouldn't be an issue. Moreover, his touch on the ball would be valued differently than when he was playing for the little British guy, who didn't really care about skill.

Well, I read somewhere that if you ever want to make God laugh, tell him your plans.

Some tryout-style scrimmages were set up. Tap would present some players with an envelope apparently containing an "offer" to play for the full Academy team. My heart sunk when my kid didn't get one of those envelopes. Guys who went nowhere near as far as my son had gone in the ODP program, were getting them. I was positive that Stefano was better than most of those kids, but I didn't know what to do now. We should have just left, but I made a big mistake. I broke my own rule. I saw myself as a more decent person than most other parents because I had never called a coach to talk about putting my son on a team before. Now, with my heart pounding I stood outside, on my driveway and called Tap Anos. I had his cell phone number because he had given it to me a couple of years before, when I asked him if he could recommend a good knee surgeon for an injury I had, a gesture for which I will always be grateful. This call felt completely wrong when the phone was ringing; it felt even worse when he answered. I struggled to explain that I was confused about my son not making the Academy team because, " he may not be able to run around like those bigger guys, but he has better feet than they do, and he'll never lose you the ball as easily as those other guys do." I thought I had made a pretty compelling challenge to the outcome of the tryouts. Then, he responded. " yeah, yeah, yeah.... I know all about his feet, but I don't think he could cover enough ground. That's my doubt. I've talked to a lot of parents over the years, and I know where this is going. So, let's go, I know I'm kind of blunt, but tell me what your expectations were. "

Expectations? Hmm. I didn't even know my expectations counted for anything- I wasn't sure what to say. "Umm, well, nothin'. I was hoping he could play for you, that's it." He said, "OK, here's what I can do. I will tell the office to put him down as a designated player. " I said, "great, thanks! I really appreciate it". I'm not exactly sure what a good definition of a designated player would be, but roughly, the designated players would train with the team, and if they managed to play in six games for the season, they would obtain full Academy status. Either way, my skin crawled. My kid had another chance to prove himself, but it felt like he was there just as a favor, and that felt like crap. Stef was tough though, tougher than I ever was, and he was going to try to make the best of this chance. I still felt some sort of revelation or reckoning headed our way and that everything would be justified.

The first few practices went really well. Stef even played in the first two games. I figured there was plenty of season left and that making the roster for four more games shouldn't be that tough. Stef kept on working hard, but things got way more frustrating and devastating one day at practice when coach Anos started calling him Stiff-ano instead of Stefano, implying some sort of lack of flexibility. I hoped it would go away, but Tap just kept enjoying the giggles that he'd get from some of the other players when he uttered this genius joke. Some of the other players turned it into Stiffy, or Stephy. Stef had to propose a physical fight to get them to stop, and then they would back down. He also got in Tap's face one day and said, "coach, that's not my name." Anos said, "ok Mr Muniz." Some of the other Dads agreed with me that Tap was a bit offsides. Others found it empowering to snicker and join in the ridicule. I was fuming. A dude I admired and considered an icon was crapping on my kid. Now what? At home my Italian wife said, "tell that asshole that if he doesn't want to play the kid, that's fine- but at least get his name right! That's it !" she said, "He's gettin' the horns!" My wife and most of her Italian family were sure that they could send evil mojo your way if they wanted. I'm wasn't so sure, but I've taken comfort in the idea more than once. To me, Tap Anos was supposed to stand for class; at least something more than disrespecting a kid who's paying thousands of dollars to be coached by him. It hurt enough that he hadn't wanted to take him, but this was pushing me way out of my comfort zone.

The whole thing was a big, negative mess. The best thing I could do, is what I should have done in the first place, just get my kid out of there before my obsessive brain could come up with any more stupid ideas.

Looking back at the way things ended with the Academy, what happened to my son was actually a blessing. Walking away from that spot that we once coveted and thought that we could not be without, actually set into motion some unexpected and wonderful events.

PS During college, at a top 10 soccer program, a fitness test was performed by the entire squad each year. It was a timed effort, including sprints and turns, designed to determine who had the capacity to cover the most ground. Stef, who had been judged by Tap Anos to not be able to cover enough ground, broke the all-time program record for the test, and it still stands today. In doing so, he outperformed many other players who were actually accepted and favored by Tap Anos.

Chapter 15: Post Academy

After leaving the NALA Academy, playing travel soccer again was lookin' pretty darn good, plus, it was easy. Stef played on two of the best travel teams in the state before going to college. The first was in the Newark area and they knew who Stef was for a few years at this point. I made a phone call and they were eager to have him. One thing about travel soccer at the late teenage years that jumped out at me (in contrast to academy ball), was how these clubs actually seemed to be playing for something. The academy structure was like a perpetual college showcase, with players playing to look good, or minimizing mistakes, instead of taking the chances that you have to take sometimes in order to win. It seemed like these Academy kids were very confident about getting onto a College team, so for them, now it was just a matter of letting the process run its course. At the Academy, wins and losses didn't seem to matter in the classic sense, it seemed like it was more about increasing the chances of getting into college. These kids from Newark on the other hand, played with passion- it was awesome to witness. When they arrived at practice, they greeted each other with a warm handshake, like fellow warriors, as opposed to the icy attitudes of the Academy guys, who seemed to look at each other as a threat to one another's futures. There had been constant bitching back and forth on Facebook between some teammates at the Academy. My son never got involved in it, but we heard it was disappointing . The Newark kids seemed like more of a team. Also, the Newark team was the most diverse team Stef had played on, it was a nice fit. There were white collar people, people who were dirt poor, white, black, hispanic, and Asian. It was mostly just Dads on the sidelines, maybe one or two occasional moms. Travel for games was not as bad. For one game in Virginia, we rented a nice bus with a bathroom, and all went down together. Of course, there had to be that one dad, a Colombian guy, who apparently wanted to take over the world. He would volunteer to coach when the usual guy couldn't be there, and then made sure he did everything to benefit himself, regardless of the instructions of the actual coach. He even refereed and played in the practices to ensure the best result for his son, (good luck trying that stuff in College), but overall, the whole experience was pretty healthy. Unfortunately, the Turnpike became the worst part of the arrangement. Getting to the practices on time in Newark was hit or miss. I couldn't leave work early enough. Then, finding parking around the field was really tough. A few times the practice area was so grid locked that I had to open the door to the truck a few blocks away, and have Stef run through the traffic with his cleats and backpack on, to make it on time. It was great that he had a place to dig in and apply his skills in a meaningful setting, but the following year we would look for something closer to home.

That fall was Stef's Junior year in High School. We figured, high school soccer, why not? At the Academy, they looked down at high school ball, but damn, it looked fun. The bleachers were full of loud people singing, and yelling. Our hometown high school team was actually really good. In fact, the previous winter, they played the NALA Academy in an indoor tournament. Manalapan High School beat the Academy team 5-0. That was ridiculous. The way people would talk at the Academy, there was no way a High School squad should be able to beat an Academy, but there ya have it sports fans, a righteous ass-kicking. The High School team wore white T shirts with numbers the guys wrote on the back with Sharpies. High school rules prevented the actual high school soccer coach from attending the game during the off-season, so the basketball coach presided over the game for the high school soccer team. Yep, a basketball coach outcoached some ex-pro soccer player in a hotly contested soccer game, featuring the 17 year olds at the NALA Academy VS a high school team made up of juniors, sophomores, and freshmen. It wasn't that hard to do- why? The basketball coach had better soccer players than the Academy. All he had to do was hand out water bottles. That's the prevailing factor- who's really better- who gets up before school to work on their game- that stuff, not who pays more for training.

Prior to the game, in the hallway, a dad from the Academy approached me and asked me where "Stiffano" was. He had been one of the turds that enjoyed rubbing in Tap Anos' brilliant joke and he wasn't about to miss a chance to project some kind of superiority. On the surface, it must have looked like Stef had relegated himself to something lower. I guess this dumb dad felt confident that he'd be on the winning side when the game was over, so crapping on somebody wouldn't bring too many consequences. Ooops. The first goal was scored by Stef dribbling through five

Academy players and pump faking the last one before roofing the ball into the net past the keeper. He ran away celebrating and screaming like a wild animal, and the ref actually asked one of Stef's teammates, "Did this guy ever score a goal before?" The ref didn't know what had just happened. The little guy who'd been bullied,-lifted some weights, turned into a muscle covered dribbling machine, and scored some sweet revenge. I got out of my seat on the bleachers without even thinking, my legs seemed to just carry me over to that dad from before the game. I leaned forward and got right in that stupid face, "wow, he really "stiffed" your whole team on that one, huh?" I left my face right in front of his, breathing hard, and as I waited for the guy to say or do something, I could sense everything about him shrinking. He did nothing. I walked past the other Academy parents from back when Stef had been at the Academy and they didn't say anything either. We were from different worlds, me, and those folks. In their world, if you can get an upper hand by just talking, you do it. In my world, words had consequences. You embarrass me, I wait, then I embarrass you, but harder. I like to think that I have matured past that type of behavior, but I have not been in a situation like that one in a long time. As the score went up to five-zero, the Academy parents looked dumbfounded. The nightmare had yet to reveal itself to them, but now, suddenly, they were living it. They had paid all that money, thinking that they were in the best possible place, and here was a high school team, wiping the floor with their asses during their last year of Academy soccer. Later, I felt uncomfortable with my petty actions, but in the moment, it was just happening by itself. Sergio Ramos, the World Cup winning, Real Madrid star once said, "soccer always offers revenge." Hello.

That was enlightening. The Academy vs High School debate had been going for a few years. People who pay between 2500-7500$ to play Academy Soccer obviously believe that the Academy is the better place to be. (I had been one of them). High school Soccer is looked at like some kind of public school, government, free participation thing. For me, here's the bottom line: if you want it bad enough, it really doesn't matter where you are playing. It'll be more about how hard you work. In the game I just described, every high school player was faster, tougher, and more skilled than every Academy player on the field. The game ended with the high school team mocking the NALA Academy by playing keep away for the final minutes, torturing their opponents, who couldn't get the ball. If we compared the collective cost of participation on the two teams, at an average yearly expense of $5000, the Academy side would have been out somewhere around $55,000. The high school side paid nothing, zero.

The following fall, Manalapan High School won the Shore Conference. It was awesome. The decision to play for the high school paid off big time. There were College scouts from quality programs at the final who approached Stef. He had never slowed down his training with the ball, and at the time, was maturing into more of a physical presence as well. On the high school team he enjoyed both the competition and recognition he was receiving by dominating the midfield. He added tons of running and weights to his routine, which also included Jiujitsu. Most importantly, he was loving soccer again, and I felt such a great relief. When things had unraveled at the Academy, I felt tremendous guilt, like I had delivered my son directly into that disappointment, and how could I have let that happen ; I had even apologized to him for putting him in the Academy. What I thought was gonna be the best thing, turned out to be really expensive, time wasting, shit. We'd left just in time.

We were able to conclude at this point; sometimes when you want to go forward, you gotta go back first. How hard you yourself are working, is the most important thing, not what team you're on or how much it cost.

I started wondering, "why would a college coach care where you had played before?," Somehow we had been brainwashed into thinking that the place where you came from was actually going to matter to a college coach. Why? What if you just showed up at an ID camp, or a tryout, and you were the best player there, right in front of the coaching staff? That's all that should matter. If you're the best player the coach's got, why should he care if you played Academy, High School, in your basement, or at the park. I equate it to the college education conversation gaining traction these last few years; Is it really worth going $200,000 in debt for a miserable job later? Well, the people paying the money will swear it's crucial. Same thing with Academy soccer, the parents paying the money to train and be part of an Academy expect a better result, but the real result comes from within the player and how hard he works to obtain it. Of course, you can get on the radar for college soccer during the high school or Academy years, and maybe get the attention of a coaching staff, but what will happen when you get to the college team tryout and your performances aren't all that good? Making sure that the game you bring to the field represents the best version of you that you possibly can, is more about YOU than the place where you learned your craft.

The last team that Stef played for before college was a local travel team that was also amongst the best in the state. It was just as good a soccer environment as the Newark team, but without having to contend with the turnpike and rush-hour traffic. Stefano's performances were getting better every week, and on a weekend when there were no games scheduled, he attended an ID camp at Rutgers University, in the bubble on the Busch Campus. He had tons of confidence, he was fit, and mentally ready.

Rutgers was high on our list because I had begun working there full-time in 2005. One of the benefits included in the compensation at Rutgers is free tuition for children of the employees. My oldest daughter had already graduated and had gone through, tuition free. I figured if Stef could make the soccer team, that would be another college tuition that I wouldn't have to worry about. After registering the players and warming up, they had the entire group of candidates sitting on the floor, and the assistant coach, Mr. Beck, proposed a challenge to the group. He took a soccer ball and started to juggle it, quick little juggles where he would be tapping the ball without putting his foot down, in what seemed like world record pace. He had one of the actual players from the squad at Rutgers, who was helping out with the ID camp, timing the whole thing. 50 juggles, 14 seconds. " anybody want to take me on?," he said. It was quiet for a couple of seconds, then Stefano said, "yeah, I'll do it." He stood up and walked to the front of the group. Meanwhile a huge sign, like a marquee at one of those old movie theaters, lit up in my head. It said, " THIS KID IS CRAZY." Click, same thing, 50 little juggles in 14 seconds. The coach had not been expecting this, - whatever his intent was when he challenged the group, I don't think he expected somebody to step up and match his freaky little gimmick. "Ok, tie-breaker!" the coach said. Was he forgetting that they had an ID camp to run? He prompted the timer guy and started again, this time, he dropped the ball almost immediately. "Ok, it's a tie, " coach Beck said. "We'll continue this later."

Stefano played great the whole weekend. He turned, controlled well in traffic, passed, dribbled, and took shots with conviction. When we were leaving at the end of the second day, the assistant Coach said, " we'll be in touch.

I told Stef not to tell anybody on the travel team about how things had gone at the ID camp. A few days later, he received the following email:

Stefano,

Thank you for attending our College ID Clinic last weekend and please give me a call to discuss Rutgers soccer into further detail. We were pleased with your efforts over the weekend and you have some upside to your game. We think you could play anywhere in the midfield either as an attacking or defensive midfielder or even out wide on the right or left flank.

Please give me a call on my cell phone to schedule a visit in the coming weeks!!!

Cell # 732-718-5562

If I do not answer for some reason please leave a message and try back again – remember I cannot call you back!!!

Thank you

Brian Grazier
Assistant Men's Soccer Coach
Rutgers, The State University of New Jersey
732-445-6225 office
732-445-5589 fax

We scheduled a visit and we were welcomed into head coach, Dan Donigan's office. A younger, assistant coach sat on one side of the desk, assistant coach Beck sat on the other side, and Stefano and I sat directly across from Dan Donigan.

Donigan said, " We wanted to talk to you today because we were very impressed with your play at the ID camp. We feel that you are what we call an "up and down player", where you can contribute to the attack but also help out on defense. We have a lot of returning players for next year so I only have one spot open, and I'm offering it to you." The coach spoke quickly, and he had a raspy tone in his speech like someone who yells all the time. I said, "He'll take it." Beck stacked up some papers, and jokingly tapped them on the table, saying "I guess we're done here!" Everybody chuckled. Donigan smiled and said, " Well, I need to hear it from him." Stef said, "Yes, I'll take it." I asked how the whole thing works when he is contacted by other schools because he had already started receiving some letters from universities that had attended travel team games, tournaments, and that very same ID camp at Rutgers, etc. Donigan said that you would just tell them that you are verbally committed to Rutgers. By this time, Donigan already knew that I had tuition remission from Rutgers because I was an employee of the University. He asked how Stefano's grades were. We responded that they were average, to which he calmly asserted that there was something called the Academic Oversight Committee, that makes sure that student athletes stay in compliance with the grade requirements necessary for participating in their sport, and that they had never denied him admittance to a player that he was interested in before, so that the only thing that Stefano should be careful to avoid would be disciplinary problems at the high school, like fighting or drugs. Donigan shook our hands, we got up, and I took off in my truck so Donigan could take Stefano for a tour of the facilities. When I picked Stef up, he told me that Coach Donigan had told him that he didn't need to be quiet about this, that he had earned this. I was ecstatic.

This would be a good place to slide in a bit of advice: I'm still not familiar with the rules on this stuff, but if you ever get news like this from a coach, you may want to contact a legal representative to "memorialize" the occasion in writing. College soccer recruiting is stacked in favor of the coach. Players can be victimized at any moment of the interaction; in recruiting, after enrollment, during the season, whatever. The coach can go back on his word, damage your chances at other schools, or just plain waste your time- as long as he appears to stay within NCAA guidelines, he wins, you lose. Anywhere else you play before college, you can leave in less than a minute if you wanted. In college, you're stuck. If you have any attachment to the academic part of the school, (which is why you should actually be there in the first place), then, it's not so easy to leave the school and go play somewhere else. You don't know if your credits will carry over, if the next school offers the type of programs that you are interested in, or what the deal will be with any tuition/scholarship arrangements. Seasoned coaches know exactly how much leverage they have over the players, and in my experience, these coaches can be pretty aggressive about capitalizing on the naivety of these incoming 18 to 19-year-olds. Pro tip: New Jersey is one of the 38 states that has "single party consent" for recording private conversations. In other words, if you are involved in the conversation directly, you are not breaking the law by recording a conversation without the other party knowing. (More on that later.)

Back on the traveling team, Stef told one person, and of course, then everybody knew. Some parents were congratulatory. The coaches however, said nothing. That travel team had four coaches, and three of those coaches had kids on the team. The one coach who didn't have a kid on the team appeared to be the head coach, in title only. Line ups were dictated by the parent coaches. That week, an email was sent out to all of the players and parents regarding ID Camps. The coaches were requesting that players refrain from attending ID camps during the season because some players from the previous year, had to wait until the season was over to go to their perspective ID camps and so it was not fair to the rest of the team, blah blah blah. I didn't care. We had done what we had to do without disrupting the team, and I started to get an inkling that there might be some resentment because of the result. My suspicion was confirmed almost immediately when they wouldn't start Stefano in the games any longer. He had been starting, he had single-handedly turned some games around, scored some great goals and provided plenty of assists. Now, he was one of the last players to get on the field, right after having been recruited by Rutgers University. Again, I didn't care. There were a few travel team games left, and Stef had already made it onto the best possible College team for our situation. I told him to just ride out the rest of the season. If the parent coaches on this local travel team were somehow butt-hurt by that, and wanted to make an example of Stefano, that was fine by me. A few more weeks and it would all be over. He would be going into his senior season of high school soccer, getting accepted into Rutgers, and so who cares.

A few weeks later, the travel team made it to the semi-finals of the state cup and was locked in a 1-1 tie against East Brunswick in a game that they should have been winning easily. Needing to win to advance to the state cup final, they decided to bring Stefano on late in the second half. He promptly stole the ball in the midfield and chipped a perfectly weighted pass over the defense, where the advancing center forward just tapped it into the goal for the game winner. The coaching staff looked so silly. They had tried to make an example of Stef, and now when they really needed to win a game, they were forced to bring him on because they knew what would happen when he got on the field. I yelled out,"Hey Stef, go back to the bench!,".and laughed. Would you believe they took him right out again? There really wasn't enough time left in the game for the opponent to score another goal, so they really didn't need Stef on the field anymore and they weren't about to let me ridicule them.

You will find that parent coaches are not easily embarrassed. You have to have a pretty stout personality to coach something you don't know anything about, but they also usually have a certain objective in mind, and achieving that objective is usually a stronger need than avoiding confrontations or getting caught doing things that are unfair. If you're lucky enough to come across a parent coach that's fair, and has played soccer before, that's a beautiful thing; I would be hesitant to let that go.

I was still nonchalant about the playing time issue on the travel team as the state cup final got closer. We had the Rutgers thing in our pocket and I figured, let those travel team people do whatever they wanted- it didn't matter.

On Mother's Day of 2014 the team was set to play the state cup final. As expected, the parent coach group did their thing, and Stef came onto the field last, when we were already losing 2-0. Whatever. You could almost understand it this time, the coaches figured there would be college scouts at a state cup final game, and playing guys who had not yet been recruited, (especially their own kids), would be a priority. On one of the first plays he made upon entering the game, Stef out ran an opponent who had taken a long touch on the ball. He slid the ball through the opponents legs and ran around him. Realizing he had lost the ball, the opposing player ran up behind Stef and, using his body like a torpedo, tackled Stef's right knee with both feet. Stef popped up into the air like he was on a trampoline. Both players took a moment to get up. When he went to try to walk it off, Stef fell down right away. He couldn't stand on that leg any longer. The referee gave the opposing player a yellow card and Stef was helped onto the sideline. He laid on the ground for a while until the game was over. Someone gave him a ride to our truck with a golf cart.

At the hospital, they put ice on his knee and said that an MRI would be required to accurately assess the damage, but there was already a suspicion of torn ligaments. On the ride over, Stefano had told me that he heard two pops when the other player torpedoed his knee.I kept asking him if he was sure that it was two pops, maybe it had been just one? "Dad, it was two," he said. I had heard that an MCL could be healed on it's own but that an ACL could not. I was already trying to minimize the damage. I started to get that nasty, swallowed a cannon ball, feeling in my stomach again. I was looking for every possible angle where this might not be as bad as it looked, but I knew it was bad. The knee was very swollen and the pain would not allow Stefano to put his foot on the floor. Every joy, we had been feeling lately, making the team at Rutgers, escaping the politics from the parent coaches, was suddenly suspended. Stef seemed to take it well. Me, I felt an anguish that changed me permanently. I blamed the coaches. I was convinced that if they had started Stef, instead of employing their manufactured punishment for doing well at an ID camp during the season, maybe the injury wouldn't have happened. More than likely, the team would've been doing better from the start of that game, instead of on their heels, getting shelled by the time they put Stef in. In fact, I had the stats to back it up. I also blamed myself. I could've spoken up when they were playing their little punishment game, but I didn't care because it was almost over. Now on the last day, everything went dark. I had that feeling in my throat that you get when you've been wronged but you think you can't do anything about it. I couldn't blame the other kid, he was just a kid, playing in a state cup final, doing the best that he could. He had even injured himself on the play. I also wondered if I was correct in blaming the coaches. There would be no way for them to know that, that would happen, but I felt like they did know that the game would be different if they weren't being so petty and allowed Stef to start from the beginning of the game. They were well aware of how different the team was when Stef wasn't on the field, but they were using their position for their own advantage, not to the best advantage of the team. Now, I felt like they got away with something that was absolutely nefarious, and not being able to do something about it was making me sick.

The insurance company had been pretty good about approving the MRI without taking a ton of time. The MRI showed that both the medial collateral ligament and the anterior cruciate ligament were both completely torn. Full MCL, full ACL. Even now, 5 years later, I can't handle it very well, and I avoid thinking about it. We contacted the surgeon who had fixed my knee in 2008. Luckily he took our insurance, the surgery would've been $30,000+. The surgery was scheduled for mid-June.

I told Donigan about what happened, I told him that the surgery was scheduled for June 12, and that the recovery period would be approximately nine months so Stef would miss his senior year of high school soccer, but should be playing again in the spring of his senior year of high school. I asked him if this would compromise Stef's spot on the team. His exact words were, "No, I would never go back on my word like that, he's got plenty of time to recover." I said, "great, thanks Coach." Then he asked me to text him the name and number of the surgeon who would do the surgery. I complied immediately, but I got a funny feeling when he asked for that information.

I mean, the guy just finished saying it wasn't going to be a problem, so why would he need the surgeon's information? Did he think I was making the whole thing up? Why would I do that? I was satisfied though, that Stef's spot was safe based on what Donigan said. Maybe he was checking with the surgeon to make sure the recovery wouldn't take longer than what I had said.

After that, I couldn't stay away from my phone. I was looking for any excuse to stop what I was doing at work, and look up information about ACL surgery, recovery, and rates of success. I think I was looking to calm down the shock of what had happened, while at the same time attacking this pile of unfamiliar things to worry about. Is it over? Can he really ever go back to playing? I wanted answers to everything immediately. Even worse, I wanted the answers that I personally wanted. I was looking for peace of mind in medical studies, case studies from other athletes, everywhere except my own mind. You can go crazy doing this, or in my case, crazier.

The procedure itself was fairly new. Apparently, it had been tried unsuccessfully with some sort of synthetic, rubber-band-like material, in place of the torn ACL. More recently, there had emerged several ways to perform the operation, each with different advantages and risks. Then, there were varied opinions on each method. 20 years before, ACL injuries meant you were done with sports. These days, there was a chance you could go back, but there was a mountain of work to do, and even then, there were no guarantees. There were some great stories out there, men and women who had torn their ACL and managed to make it back to their respective sports, but these incidences were being looked at as improbable and spectacular. Many great soccer players retired after acl surgery, unable to retrieve their form. The great Italian striker, Pierluigi Casiraghi, collided with an opponent, tore his acl, and retired in 2002, after 10 surgeries attempting to repair the knee. So now what? Stef was always pretty upbeat, (he took after his mom). Me, I realized I had to stop looking for who to blame and start focusing on the recovery. Unbelievably, I started to change my perspective, albeit slightly. I realized that it could've been much worse and I was happy to have my smiling, beautiful, son still with me. He had a good run in soccer, and maybe this was part of God's plan. If he could walk normally after this, and get around, maybe find something new; that would be blessing enough, and I would be grateful. I told myself that I had to stop thinking so far ahead. I knew that even if the surgeon did a great job, there was still a chance to re-tear the ligaments during rehabilitation, or if the rehab didn't go well, he could have a hitch in his giddy-up for life. From there, things could only get worse. I read forums about people who had five consecutive knee surgeries, there were infections to worry about, and one statistic indicated that the imbalance of muscle on the operated knee would create a dependency on the other knee, that would provoke a 75% chance of tearing the ACL in the non-operated knee. My New Yawk neighbor across the street, Tony, gave me his insight on the injury. "Ya know Bryan, maybe God's protectin' him from somethin' else...ya ask me what? Spwots, (sports), God protectin' him from spwots? Yeah, maybe, yeah. He's gonna be ok Bryan, ya know why? He's young and his body's still regeneratin'." Tony was great. He worked construction, he was not a doctor, but his opinion somehow gave me comfort and strengthened my faith. The information I was getting from my phone searches was helping me to clarify what my position should be, but at the same time, my ego kept me from relaxing. I feel like an animal, a bad parent, and really selfish as I admit this, but it's the truth- I should have been grateful that my son was in the hands of a great surgeon, that the injury wasn't worse, but deep down, I still wanted Stef to be able to play again, go to Rutgers, and also, I was still somewhat angry. I wanted to say to people who'd tried to hold him back, "you lose, my boy is stronger than your bullshit. Beat ya anyway."

In a few days, Stef got really good at walking with crutches. It was actually funny how quick he could move. One day, at a graduation party for a teammate from the academy, he started juggling a soccer ball with the injured leg, balancing himself with the crutches. His touch was still there. He hadn't had the surgery yet, but without the ACL or MCL being connected, he still controlled the ball very well with the torn up, crooked leg. I hoped that it was a sign of some divine intervention, maybe that everything would be ok, but I had to balance my hopes with the uncertainty of the next 9 months. I was afraid to get too hopeful and then feel that same pain all over again.

Chapter 16: Beast Mode

Around 2012, 2013, I started hearing the word "beast" all the time. Some guy at a pizzeria saw my heavy-duty, military grade, cell phone cover, he said, "That thing's a beast!" People's cars and trucks were a "beast". I read a book about MMA fighters, the title was, "Beast".

I know nothing about physical therapy. This is not a suggestion of how to proceed if you have a multiple ligament injury and want to make your way back into sports, but this is what Stef did, I'll call it beast mode.

From the day he got injured, Stef started training even harder than before-weeks prior to the date for surgery. We had exercise equipment in our basement and he would do many sets of dips, weights, weighted dips, and anything else that did not require his right leg to touch the ground. For cardio, he would sit in a chair and punch a heavy bag with boxing gloves on, until he had nothing left. He would sit in the same chair and pass the ball to himself against the wall with his left foot only, which was not his natural foot. He went on like this every day until the day of the surgery. He took a couple of days to recover from the surgery and was scheduled for rehabilitation less than a week later, and still he continued training himself between rehab visits. Before I continue with the recovery routine, I would be remiss if I didn't review some of the details of the surgery and the great work done afterward at physical therapy.

On June 12, 2014, while Stef was in surgery, my wife and I sat in the lobby of the surgery center, and it dawned on me, (clearly, a little late), that soccer itself didn't mean anything. In that moment, I realized that all I wanted was my son back. Not his success in soccer, not his joy from playing soccer, all I wanted was to have him back with us, back with his mother, brother, and sisters, making jokes and moving through life. Surgery, no matter what kind, is no joke. Anything can happen. Unfortunately, it took something like this to make me reflect on my priorities. At least, that's how it was for me.

A psychiatrist once told me, "Bryan, if we were all judged by our ability to play soccer, most of us would be in a hell of a lotta trouble". The game is just not that important. If you can keep that in mind, (better than I did, of course), it will help you overcome a lot of the stress produced by having your kids participate in a team sport. When we walked into the recovery area and saw Stef lying awake on the hospital bed, I had a rush of joy I'd only felt when the kids were born. God's grace and the surgeon gave me back some peace.

The surgery lasted about 5 hours. When the surgeon came down to the lobby to tell us how it went, he looked like he had been in a fight; his hair was all over the place, he was sweaty, and he seemed a bit out of breath. In the consultation prior to the operation, I had asked him if this was an easy operation. I was hoping he would say something like, Yes, standard, routine... Instead, he said that in HIS world, nothing was easy. By his appearance, he wasn't kidding. It wasn't what I would've imagined the Doctor to look like after the procedure, but the news was good, everything had gone well.

A piece from the center of Stef's patellar tendon on the front of the knee was harvested with two small attached pieces of bone from the femur and tibia. This would become the new anterior cruciate ligament. The bone blocks that had been removed with the patellar tendon would then be fastened to the femur and tibia at the back of the knee, and would hopefully, fuse with the existing bones and be accepted by the body. The empty canal left in the patellar tendon at the front of the knee would actually fill itself in over time. For the MCL, there was no place left on his own leg from which to take tendon to form a ligament, so the surgeon used a cadaver graft. This was a big thing for me- I was always reluctant to check the organ donor part of my driver's license because I was paranoid that in the event of an accident, someone may, "precipitate," my donation. Now, I was guilty of accepting something that I wasn't prepared to give before. Since then, I have become an organ donor. Another aspect of getting a cadaver graft that will give you pause, is that you get the graft from a cadaver bank where the ligaments are irradiated; this is the process of using ion irradiation on the body part from the cadaver to help prevent the transfer of infectious disease; chances are slim for a tragedy like that, but it'll still make you feel uneasy.

With every bit of extra information that I accumulated about the risks of the surgery, I always had to decide how I would explain it to my son. Would it be right to express my fears to him? Or, should I protect him? Would it be better to water down the details, maybe even lie about certain ones? Maybe he wouldn't struggle as much, thinking that everything was just routine? I took it step-by-step, and decided on each bit of info individually, hoping that I was doing right by my boy. There'd be two permanent scars, one on the front of knee and one on the side.

Another whopper in the equation was something called DVT, Deep Vein Thrombosis. A percentage of ACL surgeries result in a blood clot that can travel toward the lungs and cause something called a pulmonary embolism, which can be fatal. Even if it is not fatal, it could still prove devastating to the recovery of the patient. To help avoid deep vein thrombosis, I had to take a big needle and inject something called Lovonox into a different part of Stef's stomach every 12 hours. This stuff made him so jittery that all he could do was lay in his bed shaking, unable to sleep. The operated leg looked 1/2 the circumference of the other, because trauma from the surgery makes the muscles incapable of firing; this, added to the sudden inactivity and the bewildering loss of a big piece of his identity (being a young man who had always played soccer), caused Stefano to have some rough nights. He'd been using an App on his phone to count down the number of days until pre-season and was looking forward to another successful high school season for his senior year. Now that was gone. The high school coach couldn't look at him as he made his way through the halls on crutches. His mother told me that he couldn't sleep and he sometimes cried just laying in his bed looking at that weakened leg.

That was damn tough, and then once we got past these hurdles, there were some more long term issues that came into play.

Proprioception: The ACL that you're born with is not able to heal itself the way the MCL can. Therefore, most surgeons will opt to completely remove the ACL and replace it with a new tendon. Along with losing a piece of your original anatomy, the resulting surgery cuts through nerves and the result is a loss of proprioception. In other words, your body's ability for the brain to tell the leg what to do, becomes compromised. I have been told by orthopedics that the body will recruit new nerve endings in order for the brain to more precisely inform the body on what to do, however, this is a process that must be worked through. I believe that this is why the rate of return to sports is

157

higher amongst higher level athletes. Regaining control of the damaged leg requires an insistence on retraining the leg to do what your brain says. Not many people are willing to do this amount of work.

SCAR TISSUE- the visible scars left from the surgery- who gives a shit. There's scar tissue inside the knee left from the surgery though, and that's a different story. It has to be forcibly broken up to avoid stiffening of the joint. In physical therapy, during rehab, Amanda, the head therapist would bend the leg with Stef lying face down on the therapy table. The goal was to increase the range of motion and break up scar tissue by bringing her weight down on the bent leg. The scary part, the pain looks intolerable and gives the impression that the grafts used in the surgery are going to tear. There's an audible, cringeworthy, cracking.

Disorientation- This is such a serious injury. It takes so long to come back. For anybody who still feels young and energetic, self-doubts about whether you should go back to sports won't be hard to find.

The strength of a new ACL has been described as that of a wet paper towel. Many people have re-torn the ACL after surgery by coming back to sports too soon or even just by an unfortunate, one time mishap. It's improbable that you can follow a teenager around every day to make sure that nothing happens during the healing process. Capillaries need time to wrap around this new part of you, strengthen it, and make it yours. Thus, more anxiety.

Around that time a football player named Adrian Pedersen had made a phenomenal recovery from an ACL injury and came back the following season to break records. He credited his strong Christian faith for his recovery. I'll add this: NO FAITH?, YOU'RE DONE.

Faith, in my estimation, is the biggest part of what made Stef keep fighting for a successful result. It was emotional tonnage, and as he started to get a handle on that part, the physical work began.

The surgeon recommended JAGS Physical Therapy in Woodbridge. For the first few months, sessions were three times per week. At the beginning, I didn't think this was going to be very pleasant. The ride from Manalapan to Woodbridge was a little long, and would always be during rush-hour. Also, I thought it was going to be something like going to the doctor three times a week. It turned out to be pretty fun, challenging, and best of all there was progress every week. What made it great was the people. It was a mix of young men and women who had such a positive attitude and a confidence about themselves and their work, that we started to look forward to the ride every time and the interaction with the crew at JAGS. There was no waiting in a waiting room, you just walked right in and started to work. There was always music playing, and we got to know some of the other clients as well.

Over the months, the process seemed to break down as follows: regaining range of motion in the knee, through cracking the internal scar tissue, which as I mentioned before, was the most difficult part to watch. Regaining muscle tone was next, and towards the end, everything was focused on coordination and recapturing specific skills. On October 13, 2014, Amanda said, "treadmill today?" We laughed at Stefano's reaction, she said she'd never seen someone so excited to use a treadmill! He hadn't been able to run, or even jog in months, and using a treadmill represented a big step forward on the road back to playing. It was great to witness. No one had ever explained to me what was involved with one of these surgeries. I was completely uninformed beforehand, so to some extent I sort of looked at it like getting something fixed on your car; you take it to the guy, he works on it, and when he's done, it's fixed. You can go pick it up - and it works. This knee surgery was epic and life-changing. After the initial emotional trauma, there was a leg there that looked so weak. I couldn't wrap my mind around how he was supposed to ever play again. The operated leg looked like just skin and bones and it seemed unlikely to gain enough stability in a few months, to be able to withstand a crunching tackle from a college-aged soccer player. Amanda knew better. She measured the circumference of the recovering leg. It was making steady gains in size and strength. The surgeon, who had performed similar surgeries on several high profile athletes, told us that it was really more like a two year process. The first year you might be healed, but you won't be yourself, it's sometime during the second year, when you feel whole again. So much for the car repair idea. For Stef to play college soccer, that "two-year" concept would mean that he wouldn't be ready for his freshman year of college, and maybe have to forfeit the deal with Donigan. However, we were comforted one day when they gave Stef a lacrosse ball at physical therapy and challenged him to juggle it, like he would with a soccer ball. With the healing tendons and the shrunken leg, he did over 200 juggles on the first try, dropping the rock solid lacrosse ball from exhaustion. On the next visit, Sheldon, another Physical Therapist at JAGS, and the joker of the crew, smiled and gave Stef a golf ball. He still managed quite a few juggles. It looked like the whole proprioception problem may have somehow been averted.

That same fall of the senior year of high school, Donigan called. He said, "hey I just wanted to update you...I spoke to my contact person at admitting and they said that it's close, (with the grades). " That hit me like a bucket of cold water- because previously, he'd made it sound like disciplinary stuff would've been the only thing that could interfere with the admittance. (And there was no disciplinary stuff). I said, "Didn't you say that there was this Academic Oversight Committee, and that they always admitted any players you recruited?" He said, "Yes, and they've never told me no before, but I just wanted to let you know so we can take the proper steps." Stef needed to sure things up by improving his GPA and getting a better SAT score, (apparently), to really seal the deal. Ok. A little deviation from the celebratory, big story and quickly spoken words from that first meeting and handshake at Donigan's office, but ok. We signed up for one of those SAT prep type courses that Stef would go to every week on route nine in Manalapan. Did I mention we have four kids? With work at Rutgers, my side business, CCD, boxing, karate, jiujitsu, guitar, piano, soccer, Church, physical therapy, and now SAT prep, it was all a bit tiring- but we were talking "free college." Coffee became my best friend. I was leaving early to everything so I could stop at Dunkin' Donuts for a large or Starbucks for a venti. The number of cups I'd already had for the day didn't matter. I sat with my accountant, Henry, one day while he looked at my bank statements. He saw the debit activity for Dunkin' and he said, "Who is eating all these donuts?!" Really, it was mostly coffee, (I did have an occasional chocolate frosted donut and wake up wrap). But, it was Stef's turn to try to get into College, and we weren't about to ease up. He kept working out on his own at home (like a beast), between the physical therapy appointments. At physical therapy, they said he was the hardest worker they had ever. seen. They even filmed him in a promotional video for JAGS. The crew kept the bloopers and watched them over and over. On November

20th of 2014, Demi, another One of the physical therapists at JAGS, invented a new exercise with Stefano in mind. She called it quadrant jumps. She divided the platform on the leg press machine into four different areas with painter's tape. The exercise would be to do a one legged press and launch yourself away from the base of the leg press machine, then land in a different quadrant and proceed to rotate quadrants clockwise, then counterclockwise. This proved to be very effective because the neuromuscular connection after a trauma like an ACL tear and then the subsequent surgery, prompts the body to protect itself by restricting and minimizing involuntary muscle contractions. This quadrant jump exercise that Demi came up with, forced the muscles in the leg to adapt to a different landing in each quadrant, thereby multiplying and intensifying the muscular contractions at a greater rate than if Stefano were to use the machine in the traditional way. Stef also added an activity he called "power bike" at that time, and the crew incorporated it into the sessions. He would crank the resistance on the bike all the way up, then only pedal with the weak leg. It was brutal, it was beast mode. On December 10th, we went up to Morristown for a follow up visit. The surgeon said, "everything looks sweet." And "we're ahead of the game." Our faith was compounding after that appointment, but really, from the moment the injury happened, I felt God's presence. The surgeon who I thought had retired, was still working. After the surgical consultation, he told us that he just wanted to see my son play soccer again, that he was at a point in his career and his life where he was only working to help people. The day after the surgery my son's leg twitched by itself uncontrollably; the surgeon said he hadn't seen anything like that in 35 years. To me, it felt like God himself was putting his finger on that leg and saying, "This will be okay." The people at physical therapy said his recovery was the best they'd ever seen. Throughout the recovery period, my son never had any contempt for anyone, he showed no anger or resentment. He was more filled with faith than I could ever have been. At 17, I would have never been so full of grace. His high school number for his soccer jersey, 27, showed up everywhere. He was always pointing it out, and it was somehow comforting. After a while, we began asking what it could possibly mean. We prayed. I prayed the Rosary many times. We concluded that seeing his number was a sign from God and therefore had to mean something great.

161

Over the winter we received this text from coach Beck

Text Message
Today 10:59 AM

Hello. Hope all is well. Pls text me your runner and cleat size asap. Jersey size. Short size. Shin guard size. Jacket size. Pant size.

iMessage

Dave Beck
Rutgers soccer

iMessage

Cool, all seamed to be going well.

On February 24th, 2015, we looked up the list of new Rutgers recruits for men's soccer and Stef was not on it. He had submitted new transcripts from the high school, he had improved his SAT scores and submitted them, and so I called the coach on March 4th. This time, I had to leave a message. He did not answer or return my call. Hmm. We had been turning down other opportunities as per Dan Donigan, and now this. Being in limbo this way was taking a toll on me physically. I wasn't taking care of myself, eating all wrong, and always on edge from the stress. On one of my bi-annual physicals for my CDL license, the Doctor at work actually asked me if I had recently had a traumatic event. I didn't know it was that obvious. He noticed plaque psoriasis starting to act up on my forehead, face, in my ears, and one of my elbows looked like it was growing extra layers of skin that were there under protest, and trying to break away. I'd gained weight and bad cholesterol. This Donigan was drowning me with bullshit. I had one more card to play, a mutual acquaintance, who agreed to casually ask Donigan about Stef, and get the straight skinny. About a month later, I got my answer; my friend told me it wasn't gonna happen. He told me that Donigan thought Stef wouldn't get very much playing time his freshman year so he was gonna send him to play for Rutgers Camden. I couldn't accept it-how long had Donigan been planning this? ... and why wouldn't he let me know months ago? I let a couple of weeks go by. This kid from Matchfit Academy was in a similar situation; we heard that Donigan sent him to William Paterson. Now, in May, we were well into the spring semester. If we wanted to go anywhere else, it was past the application window for most schools, and I wasn't interested in paying 150 grand for something I could've had for free. A few days later, I texted Donigan saying that I just so happened to be working on his side of the campus, and would it be alright if I stopped by his office. He responded, "Sure, you can stop by anytime!" When we sat down he said, "Ok, I couldn't get Stefano admitted, but here's how we can salvage the situation. I already spoke to Coach (Tim) Oswald at Rutgers Camden. They have more lenient academic requirements, and he has everything ready for Stefano. There, he'll be admitted and he'll be playing with good players. Then, if he can get at least a 3.0 gpa, he can reapply here (New Brunswick), and be back for second semester, freshman year, so that he can workout with the team here in the spring and be ready for the fall, because after all, it's not where you start,

163

it's where you end up that matters." I said, "That's fine, we'll give it a shot, but I wish I'd known sooner, the suspense was awful." He said, "I apologize for that, but this is probably the best solution because you can still use the tuition remission at Camden, I mean, look at (anonymous), going to Willy P! How would you like to pay that bill?!" He smiled like it was within his power to hand out different futures to different players, no matter what he'd shaken hands on before. He had waited so long to say something, that now we had no choice, and now....I had to tell my wife...she said, "What?! Tell that asshole to send HIS kids to Camden. Piece o' shit! That's it! He's gettin' the horns!"

Looking back, I think I was so relieved that the suspense was over, that I accepted the change of plans as a welcomed resolution. I looked up Camden on YouTube. Saw a couple of public "twerking" contests. At least now I knew what twerking was. The rest of the videos about Camden were things like, "The 10 worst crime rates in the world," Camden was No. 1. Number friggin' one!

We looked at it like this; 1 semester, roughly 3 months, and he was outta there, back in New Brunswick. If he stayed in his room between classes, he could probably avoid random gunfire. Also, Rutgers Camden had been in the hunt for a national title in soccer for the last couple of years and had come close to taking the whole thing, so maybe it would be ok. I didn't care that it was D3. It would have been an issue in football or basketball, but not soccer. Most people looked at NCAA divisions like they look at European soccer, where first division is the top, then second, then third. However, NCAA divisions signify the size of the school, and budget related issues. With more lenient academic standards, D3 schools in the top 25 of the national rankings were able to admit soccer players that were good enough to play for D1, but were not eligible academically. This resulted in most top D3 teams being competitive with most D1 schools, in fact, many D3 schools were beating D1 schools in their schedule. Also, NCAA D1 schools could only have 9.9 scholarships for the whole soccer team, (for rosters that may be in the high twenties), so scholarship money got spread pretty thin, - so for example, even if you had the grades, and let's say you got a 50% scholarship to a school that was 50 grand- that would still cost almost double the in-state tuition of a smaller school with no football team, more focused on soccer. Hence, D3 schools could attract some excellent soccer players.

Camden was definitely a top 25 program, and some guys I knew who worked down there on the Camden campus, said the campus itself was well protected. Stef had not played in almost 15 months and now that physical therapy was over, he had about six weeks to get in his best shape for his freshman year of college soccer.

Chapter 17: Camden

Inside the Rutgers campus at Camden, it's not bad looking. It's a small area with concrete pathways and mature shade trees amongst the buildings. (The student center has a Starbucks); but step out of the campus, and it's depressing. It's an abandoned, gang bangin', drugged up, corrupt mess. Public servants were not serving the public, and cops were being arrested for being more criminal than the criminals. My Lawyer nephew jokingly sent me a Zillow listing for one of the many 1000$ houses for sale in Camden. Yep, a perfectly good, two story house for around 900-1000$. My nephew said we could buy one and party in it before the games.

The field sits almost directly under the Ben Franklin Bridge and there's a big fence all around it. Once you got past the feeling of looming danger though, it was quite cozy.

Stef did great in the first few scrimmages and won himself a starting position as a freshman. I felt every single tackle in my own right knee. The coach even remarked that you would never know that he'd had multiple ligament surgery. The field itself, was an unforgiving green turf carpet laid over something that was rock solid. The ball would bounce pretty high when it hit the ground, so it was actually a relief when they had away games at fields that were grass or even just a higher caliber of turf. I was becoming telepathically connected to that knee. Through God's grace, it held up fine. Stef Played in almost every game with no serious injuries. He even played in the conference final as a freshman, which Rutgers Camden won over Montclair in penalty kicks. It was a great season. Something interesting came out of that first semester in Camden though. We discovered that a significant percentage of the team consisted of players who had been recruited by Donigan, who then waited way too long to inform the players that they had not been admitted to New Brunswick. (In some cases, he just wouldn't return their calls.) Then, with no options, most players accepted going to Camden with the agreement that they would subsequently be going back to New Brunswick. It became clear to me that Donigan was passing around players to his friends and colleagues like bon bons, and not just to other Rutgers programs either. This guy was cold, reptile cold.

He was running around lying to these teenagers and then playing "catch me if you can". How he was impacting their futures did not concern him. For one of the now Camden players, Donigan took advantage that the kid lived in Piscataway near Busch campus, and went to his house with his assistant to convince the kid's parents that Rutgers New Brunswick would be the best choice for their son. Same game. The kid saw the list of new recruits the following semester and saw that he wasn't on it, called the office, and Donigan sent him to Camden. That semester at Camden, Stef had obtained the 3.0 gpa that he needed to return to New Brunswick as Donigan had stated.

This time though, when Stef called Donigan, we recorded the entire conversation.

Back In New Brunswick, Rutgers had had a successful season and the Rutgers coaching staff was awarded coaching staff of the year recognition. To summarize the recorded conversation with Donigan; he told Stefano, Ok, I'll call my contact person and get you admitted, but keep in mind that things are different now, you will have to compete for every minute of playing time. Stef said no problem, he was ready. By this time, we knew that what came out of Donigan's mouth was all shit. Sure enough, the next morning back in Camden, Coach Oswald called Stef to his office. Right there, I knew that Oswald was in on the whole ruse. I told Stef, "you know what? Let's record this too." Stef went into the meeting with his phone recording and wrapped up in his jacket, which he placed advantageously on Oswald's desk. Again, I'll remove the chit chat and just relay the gist of the conversation. Oswald told Stef that he had spoken with his "Good friend, Danny D," (Donigan), and that he had told Donigan that Stef really wasn't ready to go back to New Brunswick. Oswald told Stef that if he stayed in Camden, he would be All-Conference his junior year. On a side note, I had never known that it was the coaches who would decide which players would get post season accolades. That was a revelation. Also, as if it wasn't enough for one particular coach to have tons of leverage over an unsuspecting teenager, now there were coaches collaborating to control the destiny of the players and referring to each other like mobsters. "Oz", "Danny D." Stef walked out of the meeting without committing to anything. Like the song says "we started out with nothing, and we still had most of it left." Why did I think it was a good idea to record these conversations? I wasn't thinking in terms of evidence for some sort of legal process, that was the furthest thing from my mind because I knew it would do my son more harm than good. For all I knew, Mr Donigan and Mr Oswald were within their rights to act this way. I felt that this type of stuff was going to be hard to believe unless it was recorded. The crap that some of these college coaches get away with goes completely unnoticed, and then it's only a "your word versus mine," type of deal. I have these conversations recorded, and if anybody is helped by my presenting these facts, I know I've done a good thing.

We took the winter break to figure out what to do. Donigan and Oswald were no longer an option. We wanted Stef out of Camden and had to start considering dropping soccer and moving on without it. When we had time to reflect, the biggest question was simply this: Could all the training, driving, and surviving be for nothing?, leading you to an Oswald or a Donigan at the end? That seemed like a very poor recompense. The answer though, was yes, it certainly could, if you let it.

Chapter 18: ReRUN

First things first, Stef packed up and got straight outta Camden. Even though it was Camden, and even though we had become aware of what Donigan and Oswald were doing, it was a bit nerve-racking to up and leave. The season at Camden had been successful for Stefano, and if he went elsewhere, maybe things would be worse. It's a chance you take whenever you leave. So, Stefano left behind Camden and the other players that had been hoodwinked, and headed home after the fall semester was over. I feel a little bad talking about Camden this way, I know there are many people who proudly call Camden home, and that the community is working to pull itself up into a better situation, but if soccer was not going to be part of the equation for us, there was no reason to stay there. Back home, Stefano focused on soccer, jiujitsu, and continued his studies at Brookdale community college, which had some sort of relationship with Rutgers so that credits would be transferable. With no college soccer in the spring, it made perfect sense to continue collecting affordable credits on the comparatively beautiful campus of Brookdale in Monmouth County. It also gave us a moment to settle down and consider Stef's next move.

A big theme in what had happened thus far was that somehow, we ended up with other people deciding for us, what was going to be the path forward. (Albeit through some masterful deception). As I said earlier, in soccer, if you don't decide for yourself and come up with a scenario that you find stimulating, there are people out there waiting to "help you," and use you for their own agenda. College soccer is the Samurai master of that shit. We decided that whatever we did from this point forward, it would be based on what we, (me, my wife, and Stefano), thought would be the best thing for him. It would be a script that we would write ourselves, with end results that were worth fighting for.

That spring Stefano entered and won the 2016 New Jersey Open jiujitsu tournament. He put away sponsored fighters and even finished one match in under 10 seconds. God bless individual sports. That same spring, I strolled into the newly constructed visitor center on Busch campus where they had an office where are you could go and ask questions regarding admittance. A man named Alfred Guzzi was in charge and I sat with him for a few to discuss Stefano and Donigan, and admittance policies. He took down all the relevant information and kindly agreed to look into the matter. Two days later, I saw his number on my cell phone and answered immediately. He told me that Stefano had enough credits and a sufficient GPA for admittance to Rutgers New Brunswick, so long as the coach of the soccer team would vouch for him, but, that in the last two years, no one from the soccer team, no coach, no assistant coach, no representative, no contact person, NOBODY from the soccer team had ever reached out to the admittance office regarding Stefano. In other words, Donigan had recruited my son and sent him to Camden never intending to keep his word. Our chances of getting Stef into New Brunswick would have been better without Donigan. Other schools and options had been discarded in the process. Mr Guzzi ended the conversation by saying, "I'm sorry to be the one to have to tell you this."

I didn't even tell my wife. She had already given Donigan the horns; a double dose probably would've unleashed more bad mojo than anyone could handle.

A few days later we moved on the new plan. We even called Rider college, I had played there in college and it was close to home. That idea came to a screeching halt when my nephew emailed me a copy of a newspaper article discussing how the current coach at

Rider University had been Dan Donigan's youth coach, and how the two men were still friends after all these years. Shit. Well, at least we could cross that one off the list.

We still had one more shot at free tuition. When Rutgers-Camden played against Rutgers-Newark, I noticed that the Newark team had a nice blend of different ethnicities and that the players addressed each other respectfully, like on that Ironbound travel team that Stef had played on 3 years back. I had also heard that the coach at Rutgers Newark, Kevin East, was a good guy. Rutgers Newark Soccer though, had a quiet history; they had never won a conference championship, and were pretty much accustomed to losing to Rutgers-Camden.

In April of that year, my father-in-law had passed away at 75 from cancer. Now, my mother-in-law would be alone, at their home for the last 50 years, in the middle of

Elizabeth, New Jersey. The plan got a turbo boost. If we could get Stefano into RUN, (Rutgers University Newark), he could live with his grandmother in Elizabeth, and be 15 minutes away from the campus at Newark. His grandmother would have someone to dote on, and keep her company, and we'd be saving on the cost of housing at the Newark campus. As a bonus, what if by some twist of fate, history could be made? In the city where my parents first set roots in America, maybe Rutgers Newark could finally win a conference championship, maybe Rutgers Newark could finally beat Camden, and maybe Stefano could become the first player in history to win two conference championships on two different Rutgers schools. Oh yeah, and maybe another one of my kids would get through college for free. A full basket of things worth fighting for.

I called Kevin East. I told him who I was and that my son was playing at Rutgers-Camden and that he had left the program because Mr. Donigan had pulled a bait and switch scam, and I believed that Mr. Oswald at Camden was complicit in the scam. I told him that Stefano was entering his sophomore year and that he felt he could contribute to the attack at Rutgers University Newark, so if he were interested, Stefano was interested as well. He said that he knew who Stefano was, that he had sent us letters twice and never heard back. He said that Stefano was not the first to "go that way," (meaning, the Donigan, Oswald, shifty eyed side slide), and that he wouldn't be the last. Right there, the man already made an honest impression on me. (Kevin East was a beast). He said that having a year of conference experience under his (Stef's) belt, and winning the conference championship was huge, and that yes, he was interested.

Done.

That first season at RUN, Stef's sophomore year of college, Rutgers Newark became regular season champions for the first time ever. They broke the school record for victories in a single season, and were knocked out in the playoffs for the post season Conference Championship. They bounced back to advance to the elite 8 round of the NCAA tournament, a new accomplishment for the school. The following season, Stef's junior year of college at Rutgers Newark, the team was ranked in the top 10 in the country, also a first for the school. Now things were percolating. Kevin East would call Donigan to request a scrimmage with Rutgers New Brunswick, but Donigan would not accept.

Two more significant events occurred during that 2017 season: Rutgers Newark won the Conference championship final over Rowan, and on the way, beat Camden and Oswald. Stef had been a versatile midfielder for the two history making seasons and earned All-Conference honors. In three seasons of college soccer, he had a history making year each year.

At Rutgers New Brunswick though, things took a dramatic change for the worse. Now Donigan was also making history by breaking records; for losing.

Donigan spiraled out of control, racing week after week toward the bottom of the rankings. The post game interviews in the Daily Targum, (Rutgers Newspaper), were pure comedy.(At least, to me). I lost count of the number of times Donigan said, "To be honest with you..." "To be honest with you, blah, blah, blah..." To be honest with you... yaddah, yaddah, yaddah..." what the hell is that anyway? I can't stand that phrase. Were you planning to not be honest? Are you taking a break from your usual dishonesty to make a special effort to be honest? Should we pay closer attention this time, since you're announcing that you will not be lying? English is a third language for me, so maybe someday someone can clarify the usefulness of that phrase, but as of 2019, I stand behind my conviction that it's one of the dumbest things you can say. I remember when Donigan was really circling the drain, in one of those interviews regarding all of those last minute losses, he said, "it's almost comical that this keeps happening to us." Comical Danny D? Comical how? Like it amuses you?

Ok, long story short, Rutgers New Brunswick just kept on losing. Follow closely here sports fans, - If Donigan had admitted Stefano, Stefano would have been part of one of the worst losing streaks ever, the exact opposite of what happened playing for Kevin East. It would have been 4 years of misery and disappointment. God is good. When Stefano played summer ball with other college players, the ones who played for Donigan at Rutgers had only terrible things to say about their coach. The soccer forums were screaming for Mr. Hobbs, the athletic director, to just pull the trigger and fire Donigan regardless of how much time he had left on his contract. Some were suggesting that Rutgers New Brunswick would be better if they would just get the Rutgers Newark players.

Finally, in the fall of 2018, Athletic Director Pat Hobbs, who typically allowed coaches to finish their contracts, fired Donigan. (He still had a year left on his contract). About the only person who wasn't surprised by Donigan's sudden and overwhelming run of bad luck, was my wife, "Well yeah, I gave him da horns...and my Father's up there messin' with em too." Hell hath no fury...

Oswald who had won the NJAC with Rutgers Camden several times, hasn't even come close to winning another conference title since, and he will not have Donigan sending him players like before. During the spring semester at Newark, players touring the campus, who were on the fence regarding whether to play for Rutgers Newark or Rutgers-Camden, would ask Stefano, (because he had been on both campuses), which was better? Stefano always responded that the Newark campus, in his opinion, was better. I wonder now, if this made things a bit tougher for Oswald at Camden, when it came time for recruiting.

Before concluding on the topic of college soccer, I have to underline that not all college coaches are schmucks. Kevin East is an honest person of character, and was a blessing in my son's life. I believe a college soccer coach has an intense job. There are regulations for every step in the college coaching process and an abundance of candidates for every coaching job. I'm sure that keeping your integrity becomes a greater challenge for a college soccer coach, than in many other occupations; a guy who's successfully coaching college ball, and managing to still be a quality person, has even greater merit.

Chapter 19: Insights and Recommendations

These are my opinions only. The closest credential I have related to these topics, is being a father. Please understand that in my family, and for me and my son, soccer is a deep-rooted passion, so that our approach to participation was not necessarily based only on developing social skills, or just having fun; For better or worse, we chose to pursue excellence. The game was, and continues to be a meaningful part of our identity.

For the parents: My father had an expression that I never heard from anybody else, but the older I get, the more meaningful it has become. He would say, "Life is tough for an animal who lives inside the stomach of another animal." Soccer clubs need your player and your funds in order to exist. As a paying member, abiding by the club's policies, you are, in certain ways, being "digested" by the club. The good news is that you don't have to come out the other end as a piece of crap.

Most of the spur-of-the-moment confrontations with coaches and other parents, fail to achieve the desired result. You'll know that your anger was misplaced when you feel embarrassed at around 24-48 hours from the initial confrontation. Instead of "I'm going to take care of this right now!", try to give yourself some time to calm down and think. Believe me, whatever is bothering you, is still gonna be there in 2 days, and you're gonna want to be comfortable when you notice other team parents walking around in the supermarket. Early on, I wasn't good at this waiting stuff, and some memories still make me cringe. When I got a little better, I did the following move once; it was funny but it worked- there was another dad that would occasionally yell at my son from the sideline. I had already told one guy to shut the …. up the previous season, and I felt like I was the one who was going to look bad if I kept doing that. My son was still a kid though, and it did bother him, so now how would I take care of this without looking like a maniac? (More than before, that is). I got close to the guy at the next practice, I said, "Hey, what's up? How's everything?" I chatted with him about nothing until I was sure that my son had seen me standing near the yeller and chatting. On the way home from practice, I said to my son, "Hey, did you see me talkin' to Mr so and so? Yeah, so he came over and was tellin' me he wanted to apologize for yellin' at you. Yeah, he said that he has a nervous problem that makes him yell when he shouldn't, and he said he thinks it happens more with you because he knows that you're one of the better players, and that you're one of the only guys that could help the team win. I feel bad for the guy. He says he's on medication for it." Of course, the yeller hadn't said anything of the sort, but it put my son at ease. We all want to win. Every parent is invested in the team and you can't control everyone's emotions, but if you take a day or two, your rational mind will come up with a better idea, that will have a more lasting result. It'll be easier to look back on your kid's youth soccer time and smile, if you strategically eliminate cringeworthy moments before they happen. What worked for me was taking that 1-2 day pause when I first got stung by someone yelling at my kid, or a coach leaving him out of the game. It was better than having to apologize later for my immediate emotional reactions. One of the things that I (eventually) got right, was teaching my son a bit about human nature through soccer. As I stated earlier, a friend of mine told me to turn a negative into a positive, and instead of protecting my son from the unfair treatment from certain coaches, I took the opportunity to point out how things can actually be unfair, and together, we learned to overcome them more effectively. Soccer is a great place to cultivate skills in observation, perseverance, communication, leadership, and will power. No one will ever know everything there is to know about soccer; no pro player, no coach, or club president. As parents though, we get an opportunity to instill values in our kids as they grow in soccer. Don't overlook this opportunity while getting caught up in results and positions on the field. A college soccer scholarship will not materialize for everybody at the end of youth soccer, but if your kid ends up with more character and integrity than the average person, then every minute and every penny will have been well spent. In the cases of the celebrities who recently got caught bribing college sports coaches to accept their children into universities under the false pretense of having made it onto the soccer or rowing teams, it's obvious that the real athletes who deserved those spots were victimized by the corruption. I also believe, however, that the children of the celebrities who would have been given those spots, are the ones who's souls will be the most hollow. The real prize was not the admission, it was the values acquired during the journey of the kids that put in the work to get there on their own merit. They now carry with them, things that no one could take away, or purchase with cash.

Don't underestimate the value of pick up games. Lots of people think that all you need, is to go to the practice sessions for your team, and then the games. If you want to really get better at soccer, pick up games are fantastic. In a pick up game, a player can try new moves without having to fear being substituted for making a mistake. Many times, pick up games are more competitive and satisfying than an organized, scheduled, league game. Most recreation centers and parks have games going on all the time. There are travel team games where 4 to 6 hours are wasted in exchange for 30 minutes or less of playing time, (after adding drive time, warm up, half time, and the drive home). In a pick up game, you might get four hours of playing time in four hours! Bring a sandwich, banana, and a gallon of water. Sometimes, you'll be playing with players that are older, or just more advanced, which will provide great learning potential at zero expense.

That feeling you get when you go to receive a pass, and it's already been intercepted and gone, will wake up your awareness faster than practicing with your team, where you might be one of the better players and things are easier. You don't have to know everybody, and most people don't mind letting you jump into a game.

On Stefano's final appointment with the surgeon who performed the repairs to his knee, the great Dr Edward Decter, the Dr told Stef, "Remember, if anything else ever happens to you, it's your brain that you make your living with." Dr Decter was a man of few words, so when he spoke, I knew to take note. His advice to my son has been marinating in my mind for about 5 years, and leads me to the following recommendation; Consider keeping soccer and college separate. If it is your goal to represent your college or university on the soccer field, that's fine, especially if it helps to reduce the cost of college. Although the United States national team has won many important games with players on the field that had played in college, the opportunities for high-level soccer outside college have evolved significantly in recent years. There are now several tiers of professional soccer, several semi-professional leagues, and U-23 professional development leagues. There's also professional arena soccer and professional Futsal. I mention this because the rigors of the college soccer schedule may be detrimental to good study habits. The college soccer schedule involves a ton of traveling and exhaustion. The number of games played in a college soccer season is not a natural rhythm for competitive soccer. Twenty- (or more), games in less than three months is pretty taxing on the body and leads to many overuse injuries, even for players who don't play the whole game. Injuries that set you back for one or two weeks could result in missing 6 games within that short time. By merging soccer and study within a one semester time frame, which ends up being 4 of the 8 semesters for a 4 year degree, a player may end up not prospering in either; the soccer affecting the studies, or the studies interfering with soccer. Yes, you can manipulate the fall schedule, but those credits will have to be made up some time in the future and may represent yet another stressful overload. Also, if you love soccer, you might find the freedom (outside of college), of being able to leave one organization, and try out somewhere else, to be more valuable than playing for your college because you may find scheduling to be more flexible, or an outside organization that is a better fit.

"Spare parts and broken hearts...keep the world turning around" Bruce Springsteen

In soccer, it's not "IF" you'll get injured, it's when.

Make the most of your time when you're injured. Train and eat in the healthiest way that you can while you're out of the game. Use the time that you would spend zoning out on video games, to watch soccer, analyze better ways to play, and investigate better ways to think, for when you go back to playing. Many people don't come back to sports from injuries like the ones my son had. Coming back to soccer AND moving up a level from high school to college, was a medical anomaly. Yet, with faith and focus, it only took a piece of the front of my son's knee, resituated in the back, and a dead man's ligament, (for which we are profoundly grateful), for him to become a two time, college conference champion with All-Conference honors. You can come back from serious injuries better than before; it's a God and mind thing.

"If you live for someone's approval, you'll die from their rejection." Lecrae

If you love soccer, and you know in your heart that you're good, never accept a negative outside opinion. My son kept going even when some experts didn't believe in him. He ended up achieving more than the players who those experts placed above him. On a few of the away games during college, he was greeted after the game by players who had been placed above him back at the Academy, full-fledged, envelope toting, Academy players. They had been spectators at Stefano's game, because they had not been able to make their college teams. Months earlier, (world class) experts, had gotten it completely backwards. I placed way too much belief in experts. Most of the time, they ended up being about as accurate as a walrus throwing a dart.

There are thousands of even more extreme examples. Here's a good one: Carly Lloyd got cut from ODP 4 times. She became one of the best women's soccer players of all time, captain of 2 of our World Cup winning national teams, and scored the game winner in two different Olympics to win gold for the USA. Good thing she didn't stop playing soccer when she was told she wasn't good enough. Consider each criticism, decide if it's going to help you, then, adapt and move on. If you keep working on soccer, you can only get better. No one can know what changes will occur in your mind and body that might help you later. YOU decide when you're done.

I touched upon this slightly earlier, but undeniably, there are some personality types that lend themselves to team sports better than individual sports. You can save yourself a ton of time and money if you carefully decide which one fits better for you or your player. My recommendation here is to become involved in both, and then gravitate toward the one where your kid really lights up the most, (regardless of whether it is a scholarship sport or not). I was raised on soccer, but through my children I realized that there are things about individual sports that soccer cannot provide. Also, there are details about being on a team that may stifle potential in certain personality types.

The efforts of a kid who is focused and trying to do his best at soccer, can be derailed by teammates that spend practices talking about video games, or whose parents are using soccer as babysitting, leaving the more committed player de-energized. I've seen kids who strive to improve at every practice, having to do drills with another player whose main objective is to ruin the drill, and laugh at their own lack of discipline. Although these types eventually remove themselves from the team, they are still taking something away from the kid who puts his heart into every drill. If the more intense kid applies that same focus toward an individual sport, he may feel more satisfied with his results, with nobody dragging him down. I know this seems very obvious and logical in writing, but in real time, there's a tunnel vision that can take place that can have you stuck in the wrong environment, wasting time better spent elsewhere. Kids can feel obligated to their parents, or even their friends, making them stay in the wrong place, hesitant to make a change. For us, what eventually worked were calm, private conversations, moving closer to a settled feeling.

Try, as a family, to stay focused on the enjoyment of playing soccer. During my time as a soccer parent, I got off of the healthy path a few times. I became focused on making things right when I thought there was an injustice toward my son, or proving my point about soccer. It was what my ego demanded, but it's way too big of a job. Now that I've had time to reflect, I realize that most of the effort to unveil the truth was a waste. I had occasional moments of satisfaction, but nobody has ever called or written me to say, "Hey, you were right." Or "I get it now, I apologize for my nearsightedness." It's a team sport, but the most important thing is what you and your kid get out of it. I envy the families who always seemed to be calm and content even when things were not going their way. They had that precious peace that is a bitter struggle for other people to acquire, and they made it look easy. You can choose to celebrate improvements over yelling about disappointments. Remember that you alone will be stuck with the repercussions. I do regret not having done a better job with communication, both internal and external.

If you're considering a college soccer program, talk to people around the program about the tendencies of the coach. If the guy is a decent human, most current players will know. I used to think that the coach of a college program must definitely know what he's doing and that his decisions will always be in my kid's best interest. Now I know better. Some inquiry regarding the coach or the program might save you some unnecessary strife. I found the following example to be pretty interesting: one college coach would repeat the same exact move every year- one or more freshmen would get a starting spot right from the beginning of preseason scrimmages. The freshmen would be thinking, "Hey, this is great, coach must really like my work. I've been playing well, and the coach noticed." This will bother upperclassmen who were expecting to walk right into a starting job, feeling confident that they've paid their dues. Now, they find themselves coming in off the bench, apparently outdone by the freshmen. Right there, there's a big win for the coach. The upperclassmen have to exert more effort to earn that spot, which looks to be in serious danger of vaporizing. Their options are limited. Switching schools during junior or senior year may be too risky or just undesirable. The upperclassmen will have to work hard to gain the coach's respect, quickly. One or two games into the season, with the upperclassmen desperate to recapture their status, the coach will suddenly bench the freshmen. Now all the fish are on the hook. The upperclassmen know that they best not step out of line, because they can easily be replaced. They know damn sure who is in charge. The bewildered freshmen have had a taste of the starting lineup and they're not sure why they're not starting any more, but they feel like they can get it all back if they just work a bit harder. It's a pretty disingenuous move by the coach, but he can pull it off every year because most players won't transfer under these circumstances, thinking that they're this close to getting what they want. Other coaches are more sincere, (maybe they had a better upbringing), but wouldn't it be nice to know this stuff before you commit to a program? There are an endless amount of coaching tactics that you might find unacceptable; buzz around and try to get the inside scoop.

Some coaches make it a point to not "bury" players that they've recruited. So, even if the player is new, he still gets a chance to prove himself and win a legitimate spot in the starting line up or earn significant playing time. Other coaches lure the players in with promises of playing time and then keep them on the bench for 4 years or until they quit. In colleges that don't pride themselves on soccer, coaches can hide out until retirement without even trying to have a winning season, so long as they manage to continually recruit enough players every year who will pay the tuition. Eg. 30 players X $50,000 = $1,500,000. That's revenue brought to the college through the coach. At many schools, the salary for the coach of the soccer team will be less than $50,000. (Payscale.com). So, it's conceivable that (under certain administrations), the record of the team every year could fade into the background, so long as the coach manages to continue to obtain players, and generate a good return on investment for the school. Because of the limited scholarship potential, most of college soccer becomes a "pay to play" transaction, or in some less favorable circumstances, "pay to not play".

NCAA.org is a great resource for information on recruiting and all other rules for Collegiate sports. Familiarize yourself with these rules to obtain a better understanding of how and why coaches make decisions. I was surprised at the number of times I've seen a player get recruited for college soccer, and then get little or no playing time. However, NCAA regulations call for sports teams to maintain a certain grade point average and college coaches receive bonuses related to their compliance with this rule. Then I discovered that sometimes a player was recruited just to boost the GPA for the whole team, while the other guys get to actually play. Things like that never occurred to me as my son got closer to college soccer. Looking over some of the NCAA rules may help parents to ask the right questions of perspective programs for their kids. A buddy of mine had a son who was recruited by a D1 program in Pennsylvania. He cheerfully invited me to go watch his son play whenever the games were nearby and I agreed. That phone call never came. My friend explained to me later, that in four years of college ball, the kid played for three minutes once at an away game, that was it. Really sad. Neither one of us knew about this "team GPA" business, but maybe my friend would've made a different decision if he had a better understanding of the situation beforehand. Of course, this is just one example of how NCAA regulations affect student athletes. There is a due diligence for student athletes and their families that you don't hear many people mention,l until it's too late.

Stefano is now done with college. He studies Brazilian Jiu Jitsu, trains youth soccer players, and accepts 1 on 1 challenges in soccer. The Soccer journey was more difficult, more dangerous, (both emotionally and physically), more expensive, and more taxing overall, than what I expected. The question that was waiting for me as this youth soccer journey wound down, was this; what are the guidelines by which we decide if this was all worth it? Outwardly, the body of work appears to be quite generic. If you put my son's soccer adventures on a resume, the average person would lump him in with everyone who participated in youth sports at any level. In the current political climate, making Region 1 ODP, and coming back from 5 hours of multiple ligament surgery to be an All-Conference Collegiate Athlete, would probably get the same attention as being the captain of intramural team frisbee. Looking from that angle, it wasn't worth it, (actually, that would be somewhat depressing). The real answer is internal. Inside you as a parent, and inside your kid. As you watch the trophies, plaques, picture frames, and medals start occupying more space in your home, you may start to believe, as I did, that this should all lead to a path of easy acknowledgement and recognition, and that this manifestation of success is the actual reward.

Fortunately, there's more to it than that. Having had time to step back from the teams, games, practices, etc., I find that the most pronounced and undeniable acquisitions come from what my son now knows about himself. He knows that he can be an outlier, on the wrong side of the age, and growth curve for sports, and still compete and do well. He knows that he can overcome politics because he outlasted and outsuffered others that tried the easy way. That's really important. He knows that he's capable of overcoming injuries that end careers for most athletes who try to come back to their former level. He knows that he even moved up a level after those injuries and prospered in two different sports, and that the list of people who've done that is really short. Sure, you can tell your kids that they are limitless, but there's a big difference from you telling them, to them knowing it without a doubt. That's what the pursuit of excellence provided for my son, and that is why it was worth it. I wish peace and the best of luck to all parents and children on this journey.

Afterword

I want to use this part of the book to say how blessed I am to now be coaching and training youth soccer players. I want to give a special shout out to the Titans family. I am blessed to work with the team and watch all the kids grow up. I want to give a shout out to everyone who trains with me inside of Stefano's Training Systems. All the players and families I get to interact with through soccer mean the world to me and give me passion and purpose to become better everyday.

Stefano's Training Systems is the soccer company I run in central Jersey. Training players and watching them develop gives me purpose and is how I express my passion for soccer.

The first year I was able to start training The Titans, we started off in a lower level National League. The second year we moved up to the second highest National league, and went undefeated. The Third season we grew to three teams: one EDP team and two national league teams. All three teams were top competitors in their leagues and took either third place or higher. Starting from the beginning, and with nearly all the same players we started with, and without cherry picking players from other teams, the Titans have developed into a group of disciplined players with great playing ability.

This part is for a story or two that did not need to go in the book, but it definitely portrays some poetic justice.

Remember that Mallet character from the beginning of Part II of the book?, This next part is something that must've come from a higher power. Between college semesters, there are college level summer leagues. As fate would have it, the team that I was playing for, called UFA, had to play against Mallet and his son's team in order to win the league. The game starts off and I was able to get an assist pretty early on in the game. The game went on to be really close at the end, until I received a pass, and was on a breakaway. The other team's goalie came out to stop me, I dribbled around the goalie and one defender before calmly pushing the ball into the net. To celebrate what turned out to be the game winner, I went over to the corner kick flag and put it between my legs and shook my hips back and forth. As the celebration took place, Mallet began to yell, "That's a red card!" The referee gave me a yellow card, and so that there wouldn't be any physical altercations, my coach subbed me out after the goal. As I walked past the other team's bench, I had the opportunity to speak to Mallet and say, "I know you like that, don't act like you don't." That game ended up being the deciding match, with UFA coming in first, and Mallet's team coming in second. Once again, I was blessed to have the opportunity and preparation to disprove the conclusions reached by Mr Mallet earlier in my youth soccer journey. This was just one game, but it meant the U-23 championship, and represented the final opportunity to make a statement on Mallet's own home field and serves as just one more example of pushing forward despite what other people may think.

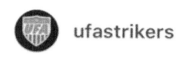

This is the summer league team, UFA Strikers, I played for and beat Mallet's team with to solidify another title in my soccer career.

As I, Stefano, was writing this book, I would go to a local Whole Foods to write. On one of the days, I look up and Tap Anos was walking by. I said to him,"Hey you're Tap Anos, do you remember me?" He replied ,"Yeah I think I do, what are you up to?" I could tell he hadn't remembered me. I told him, "I'm writing a book about soccer." His response was really telling; "That's great you are still in the business." Still in the business? That sounded strange to me. I'd never considered looking at soccer that way. It could be that he was just making small talk, but in this minute long exchange, I was able to appreciate some profound differences between my own youth soccer experiences, and the experiences that I aspire to provide for the players that I work with now, and in the future. Here's me, writing a book about soccer in a Whole Foods that this man was a big part of, and there he is, not even knowing who I was, less than five years after being my coach, after growing up playing in his academy. If my recollection about a kid who played for me, who"d paid me thousands of dollars a year, for almost 7 years, ever got this slippery, I would have to wonder if I"d been involved enough in my occupation, to justify the cost of my services.

Incredibly, less than a month later, a similar incident occurred. I was coaching inside an indoor soccer facility that had multiple clubs renting at the same time. I looked over to the next field, and Dan Donigan was coaching at the field next to mine. I told my dad, "Oh man, this is too good to pass up." I walked over to Donigan and opened up a dialogue. Once again, someone who I'd dealt with extensively, who had tried to decide my college choices for me, had no clue who I was. Roughly, three years had gone by. During the chat, I asked, "How's Rutgers doing?" he said, "I'm not there anymore, they fired me." After that, I closed the dialogue and went on to coach a better practice than he did. Again, be it soccer, or anything else in life, I'll remember these events, and strive to provide something more human, more genuine, and not so "business" oriented.

The Journey In Pictures

Father, Bryan Muniz, getting Stefano, son, ready for the world of soccer starting off with the fundamentals.

Stefano, with the cool hair he had seen on TV. My parents were always a hundred and ten percent supportive.

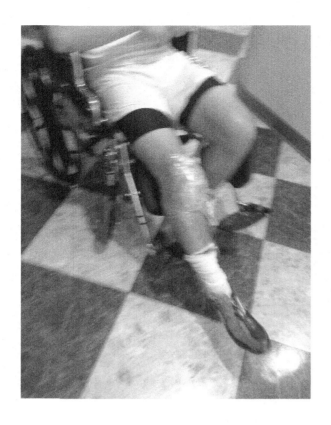

I still remember my mom asking,"Stef it's Mother's day, why not take one game off?" Happy Mother's day, two damaged ligaments later. Love you Mom.

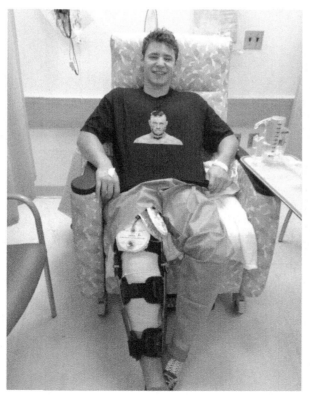

A half hour after surgery. At the time, my favorite UFC fighter was Conor Mcgregor. We had the same knee surgery. During an interview he stated,"I celebrate adversity." I took that with me as I battled to come back to playing soccer.

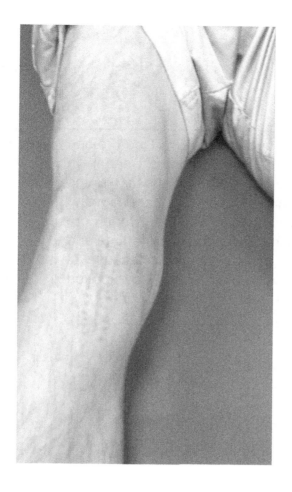

The first time they took all the bandages and I saw how small my leg became I began yelling to my Dad,"Dad my leg! It's practically gone something must've gone wrong during surgery my leg is too small!" He replied calmly,"What are you worrying about? You start walking around and the leg comes back. Don't scare me for no reason." I don't know if I was naive or just wanted some hope, but the "walk around and the leg comes back" trick was enough for me to feel alright in that moment.

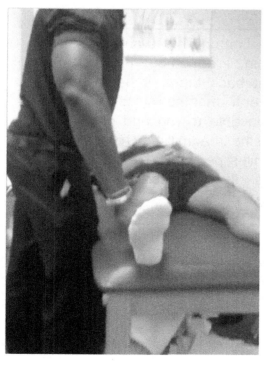

Physical therapy was a constant battle between having hope and having to face where I was. I had God and my family on my side the entire time, which gave me enough power to come back. The physical therapy crew that helped me come back did such an amazing job. I'm very grateful that I had them to help me through this hard time.

I couldn't use my legs much during the 6 months I spent on crutches. I spent those months lifting weights and just imagining the moves I would do when I got back. It was the summertime and I would wear pants because of how small my leg looked compared to the other one.

The first day I was able to run again, I remember having to fight back tears. It had been several months since I had been able to run and on that day the treadmill may have said 5 miles per hour, but to me, I was flying towards playing again.

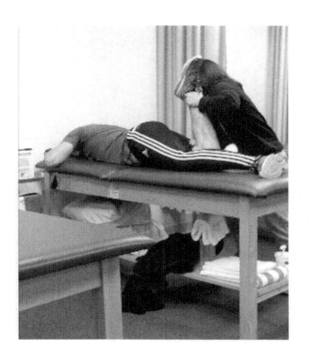

During physical therapy, they needed to break up scar tissue inside my knee, which meant bending my knee as hard as they could while I tried not to yell at the top of my lungs.

This was my first game back in 2 years due to injury. I started for Rutgers-Camden as a Freshman. It was a tough season for me. I had to still get back to my level of playing, but I still managed to start several games, and play in the Conference final where I won my first NJAC.

After my freshman year at Rutgers-Camden I went to community college and started studying Brazilian Jiu-Jitsu. A week after I earned my blue belt, I competed in the men's middleweight division of the NJ Open tournament. I won and even beat a sponsored athlete who took third in Europe. Not bad for someone who is using ligaments that aren't theirs.

This was taken from the Pre-Season camp for Rutgers-Newark the fall after I won the NJ Open. It was a funny environment, being that I came from a rival school. In the beginning I was isolated and even got told,"Go back to where you came from if you're going to play that hard at practice." I replied, "I'm here to win the NJAC, not to lose."

This was taken after I scored in the sweet 16 of the NCAAs. I scored and had an assist in the first 27 minutes of the game against the team who knocked out Rutgers-Camden the year that I played there. The ball was bouncing around inside the 6 yard box and I came through blasting it in.

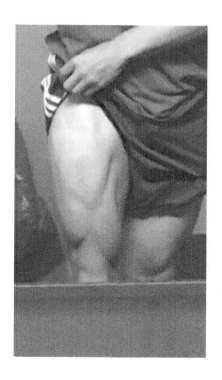

2017 Pre-season Camp I took this picture. It was an individually satisfying moment to see I had gotten my leg back after all that hard work I had to go through. With God all things are possible.

This was after scoring against a top 25 team for Rutgers-Newark. At the time I thought it would be funny to celebrate as if I was saying,"What do you want me to do?"

D3SOCCER.COM
TOP-10
1. CALVIN
2. TUFTS
3. CHICAGO
4. TRINITY
5. LYCOMING
6. RUTGERS-NEWARK
7. AMHERST
8. ONEONTA
9. JOHN CARROLL
10. HAVERFORD

During my time at Rutgers-Newark we were constantly in and out of the top 5 in the country. Had Dan Donigan let me go to Rutgers- New Brunswick I would have been part of the worst Rutgers-New Brunswick team in history.

After winning my second NJAC I grabbed the trophy and went right to my Dad and brother. One of the parents of another player hopped in the photo. They say the grass isn't always greener on the other side, but this time that couldn't have been more wrong. I was an all conference player, a 2 time NJAC champ, and the only player in history to win the NJAC on the 2 different Rutgers schools.

This is the ring all the players received after winning the NJAC for the first time in Rutgers-Newark history. Grateful to be part of that history making season.

If you've got a fighting chance, always choose to fight, you might win a bunch of things and make history.

This is my father, Bryan Muniz. He's 53 years old in this picture. He still plays (post massive heart attack) and wins championships. I grew up watching him play and to this day, I still haven't seen a goalie catch one of his shots.

Two days after Rutgers' men's soccer season ended with a loss to Wisconsin in the Big Ten Tournament quarterfinals, Dan Donigan was let go as head coach on Tuesday.

"After an evaluation of the program's performance, a change of leadership is appropriate at this time," Athletic Director Pat Hobbs said in a released statement. "We are very thankful for Dan's dedicated service to Rutgers and its student-athletes. He contributed to our rich history of soccer success. Moving forward, we are committed to securing a head coach who will help our student-athletes compete and succeed at a Big Ten and national level."

Rutgers is beginning a national search immediately.

Rutgers fires men's soccer coach Dan Donigan

By Rich Fisher For The Trentonian   Nov 6, 2018
Comments

Former Rutgers University men's soccer coach Dan Donigan, right, watches the Central Jersey Group III playoff game between Steinert and Hamilton last fall. Donigan was hired as boys soccer coach at Notre Dame High on Monday. (Kyle Franko/ Trentonian Photo)

< Back   **+ Post New Thread**

 RUnTeX
All Conference

Every day that goes by is a day lost in the traction and momentum that a new coaching staff could be gaining with respect to recruiting and implementing their system, culture, etc. This is truly a sad state of affairs for Rutgers Soccer.

C'mon Hobbs....just do it!

Nov 15, 2017   65

< Back   + Post New Thread

 All American

2nd round or not 2 years ago, he hasn't won a
B1G game in 2 years. He lost 6-2 to the 2nd worst
B1G team at home in humiliating fashion in his
8th year as HC. Would you at least acknowledge
the fact that coaches in his position should be
terminated? Because frankly, you sound like a
Floodie around this time 2 years ago defending
Flood.

Nov 15, 2017   79

If Donigan doesn't get fired, this is the classic example of why our sports programs have always been poor. We always do things on the cheap. Then when it's time to cut bait, we wait a year or two too long. So instead of digging out of a small ditch, we are climbing out of a giant crater. There is absolutely no reason for him to not get fired. None.

I can't see how he would still have 3 years left after this year. Counting this year that would make 4 and last year would be 5. If we gave him an extension before last year that gave him 5 years total at that point, then our administration should be up for a public flogging in the middle of Yurcak Stadium. This program should be a top 15 team annually with all of the talent in NJ, Eastern PA, NY and MD. Absolutely terrible where we are at at this point. Pay the guy off and get him out. Start acting like a B1G program.

Nov 15, 2017   64 ❮

Rutgers-Camden Offers Slightly Cheaper Out-of-State Tuition: ($28,890 USD vs. $28,987 USD)
Rutgers-Camden Provides Much Better Freshmen Financial Aid: (95% vs. 81% of Eligible Freshmen Receive Aid)
Rutgers-Newark Students Graduate More in 6 Years: (67% vs. 55% Graduation Rate)
Students at Both Institutions have the Same Median Post-Graduation Salary: ($54,500 USD)
Rutgers-Camden Has Slightly Smaller Class Sizes: (12:1 vs. 14:1 Student-Teacher Ratio)
Rutgers-Camden Has Slightly Hotter Summer Weather: (77 degrees Fahrenheit vs. 75 degrees Fahrenheit)
Rutgers-Newark Has Slightly Colder Winter Weather: (34 degrees Fahrenheit vs. 38 degrees Fahrenheit)

you forgot to add the one about Rutgers Camden having 6 NJAC Championships to Newarks 0.
Newark is also 2-10 in the last 12 games against Camden.
Could also argue Camden is a much safer campus

 Logged

Re: NJAC
« **Reply #11 on:** September 26, 2017, 06:16:40 pm »

Looking forward to the most intriguing match of the year in the NJAC: Rutgers-Newark v Rowan. I think it will come down to this game to decide who wins the NJAC this year.

Rutgers-New Brunswick is struggling dearly in the Big Ten, maybe they could use some kids from the Rutgers-Newark team!

Skills   Passion   Execution

For soccer training inquiries in New Jersey, you can reach me

at

stefanostrainingsystems@gmail.com

@stefanostrainingsystems on instagram

Stefano's Training Systems on Youtube and Facebook

Made in the USA
Middletown, DE
26 September 2020